
BUT FIRST, YOU MUST FORGIVE

TONI GIDDLEY

BUT FIRST, YOU MUST FORGIVE

Finding your true motivation from within and becoming your best self after tragedy and loss

By Toni Giddley

ISBN: 9798683906436

Copyright © 2020 by Toni Giddley

Cover design by: Sooraj Mathew

Edited by Hilary Jastram

STAY IN TOUCH

– Follow me on Facebook at Toni Giddley.

– Join my private Facebook Group, *Restore Life Today.*

– Instagram @Toni_Giddley

– www.ToniGiddleyLifeCoach.com

*This book is dedicated to the five
beautiful children I was not able to
bring into this world. And to all the
women who have survived loss,
abuse, and mental beatdowns.*

It is our time to empower ourselves!

But First, You Must Forgive

*Finding your true motivation from within and
becoming your best self after tragedy and loss*

By Toni Giddley

CONTENTS

As children, we all have dreams about what we will be when we grow up. Some know the second they say the question out loud. Others change their minds so many times they lose count. They walk so many paths that they end up getting lost.

We enter a life that we didn't want.

We make choices that we can't change.

We have actions done to us that we can't forgive.

The difference between those who move forward and those who become stuck in the same routine is, those who move forward learn to forgive.

Saying "I forgive you" does not mean the person who hurt you has no responsibility for their actions.

Forgiveness is not about the other person. Forgiveness allows you to become free and gives you peace.

It is for this reason that I went beyond forgiving to creating courses that will allow you to forgive as well. There is such power in forgiveness, and you owe it to yourself to learn about it and how to use it in your life.

Healing From Emotional Trauma is one course that I created that gives you an understanding as to what the words "I forgive you" truly mean. I created it because when I learned to forgive, it changed my life and got me unstuck.

Forgiving was one of the hardest lessons I had to learn.

It took me over six years of working on it—while living a destructive life—to finally forgive my abuser, the man I trusted to protect me and be at my side—my husband of eighteen years.

Through my journey, I also had to forgive God.

Some might find this controversial.

But I wouldn't be honest if I didn't say that for every baby lost, every punch I took, and every day I withstood the emotional abuse, I blamed God.

To move forward and become the most elite version of myself, I had to forgive Him.

Healing From Emotional Trauma came from my experiences. In the numerous modules and lessons within those modules, I share why forgiveness is needed to help you release your anger and pain.

Once I discovered forgiveness, I naturally wanted to show anyone how they could become their beautiful self. Thus, the course, Becoming Your Beautiful Authentic Self was created. This particular course touched all the aspects of my life. As I was creating it, I discovered new joys that came from forgiving. I then felt even more of a shift coming from my body and mind.

As you shift, you also will begin to understand that you have to live YOUR life, not the life others think you should. And you have to live your life as the real YOU.

All of my courses are geared toward helping you become the best and most elite version of yourself. They will help guide you whether you are starting your life over or are ready to take your dream to the next level. Together we can accomplish anything with hard work, determination, and the right mindset.

YOU will become the best.

YOU will get through your current obstacle.

YOU are worthy of having it all!

CHAPTER 1

What's for Dinner?

*"The thing about romance is people only
get together right at the very end."
—Sam from the movie, Love Actually*

When I got in the shower, a stabbing pain went through me and doubled me over. I grasped my belly, bent at the waist, and shut the water off. Still in pain, I tried to wrap my towel around me. Being that I was wet, I was trying not to fall and slip out of the shower. I hobbled over to the bedroom and crawled into bed. That's when I felt a shoulder pain like a knife slowly going through my muscle and into the bone.

From reading one of the chapters of the book *What to Expect When You're Expecting*, I knew I was having pain from an ectopic pregnancy. A lot of times, a woman might feel ectopic pregnancies happening in their shoulder. As I read the book, I remember thinking, *how weird, your shoulder? Really?*

1

And there I was, experiencing that pain, alone, shivering, hiding under the covers hoping I was wrong, but knowing in my heart, I was right.

When I was twenty-seven, my husband Richard and I found out that I was pregnant.

We met when I was eighteen years old and started our first business when I was twenty-one.

We had talked about having babies extensively, but I wanted to wait, and so we waited. I stayed on birth control pills, and we built our first house on an acre of land, in a town called Grizzly Flats, in California. Then we dedicated the land to growing weed illegally.

Our house was special. We designed and built it ourselves, rented heavy equipment, graded the land, put in our own electrical, and completed every nook and cranny of it. On the weekends, our friends would help us. One guy who was a roofer helped us roof the house. Another worked in construction, as a construction manager for a big commercial builder, and he framed every wall. It took us a year to build it, so we were very proud of our first house when it was done. We were only twenty-six.

A year later, I was pregnant.

Richard and I had talked throughout the years about how many children we wanted. I was an only child, and he was partly raised by his grandparents, who called him their youngest of thirteen. He wanted a big family. I just wanted more than one child because I had been lonely growing up. As a child from a military family, we moved around, so keeping friends and having friends was difficult to do.

When we found out that I was pregnant, we were very, very elated. He cried. I cried. We had been trying for about six or seven months and finding out I was expecting was a joy. In that moment, we felt we had everything going for us. We had finished building our first home. We had sold our first business. I had just gotten my real estate license since I had fallen in love with the industry. He had just gotten a small business license to open up a construction company. Everything was going our way.

The minute I found out I was pregnant, I bought three or four pregnancy tests and peed on them at different times throughout the day just to assure myself that I was really pregnant. Then I bought the book, *What to Expect When You're Expecting* and read it in two days. I sat there on the recliner in the living room with our dog next to me, reading everything I could about being pregnant. I didn't move as I made sure I knew exactly what to expect, what to eat, what to drink, and when to make my first doctor's appointment. I even wrote down notes. I was going to be prepared and ready.

I made an appointment for my first OB-GYN check scheduled out about six or seven weeks from the time I found out I was pregnant. As we got closer to the time when I would see the doctor, I was very careful about everything, and I was never told I was a high-risk pregnancy. Still, I was scared. This was my first baby.

One morning, I got back from my morning walk with the dog, returned home, made myself some breakfast, and read the newspaper a little bit. I love to read the newspaper in the morning.

When I was done reading, I got up to take a shower and prepared to go down the hill and grocery shop and run other errands. Grizzly Flats was up in the mountains, so it took a good forty minutes to get down to the big town.

When I had that cramping on my right side, was curled up in a ball rocking back and forth, and felt the pain in my shoulder, that chapter popped into my head, and I thought, *is this an ectopic pregnancy?*

The pain was one like I had never felt. It wasn't a pulling pain. It wasn't a pushing pain. After lying there for a good half hour, the pain seemed to stop. I checked the mattress for blood, and there wasn't any. I went to the bathroom, and there wasn't any. The cramping was gone, too. I got dressed and decided I wasn't going to go down the hill that day. I would just stay home and rest.

I tried to relax, but I kept reading that chapter over and over and over again. At one point, I had to tell myself to stop because I constantly wondered about it. When my now ex-husband came home, I told him what I'd felt, and he said, "Well, let's see what's going to happen. Give it until tomorrow." Then at dinner time, as we were watching TV, I felt that dull pain in my shoulder, and the stabbing pain I'd had in my stomach that morning came back. It wasn't as brutal as it had been earlier, but I started feeling it and told him about it. He said to me, "Oh, there is no way that this has got to be good."

So I called the after-hours number and made an appointment to see my doctor the next day. When I hung up the phone, I turned to look at Richard, who was in the kitchen, making himself a snack. I said, "You're going to come with me, right!?" He turned to me with a puzzled look on his face and said, "No, I have to work." My eyes welled up with tears, and I softly pleaded, "But this is a very important appointment. What if I don't have the baby anymore? What if this is the ectopic pregnancy I was telling you about?" His voice turned stern, "You'll be fine. When I get home for dinner, we'll talk about it." With tears now rolling down my cheeks, I told him, "I don't want to go to this doctor's appointment by myself." Richard, fully facing me now, raised his voice, extremely irritated, and snapped, "I said, you'll be fine. Stop your crying."

The next day I went to the doctor's appointment by myself. They had me take a blood test that tells you where your hormone levels are. If you're pregnant and the pregnancy is viable, your HCG numbers will double the next time you take the test. So I got that blood work done, and the next day, I had to come back at the same time to get my blood work done again. I was so anxious to see the results. The doctor explained to me that the numbers had to double, and if they didn't, then there was a problem with the pregnancy.

After that second blood test and once home again, I anxiously waited. I paced. I went for walks. I kept checking the phone to make sure I could hear a dial tone. I constantly waited for the phone to ring. Every two minutes, I looked at the clock, and it felt like an hour had gone by.

Finally, that afternoon, I got the phone call. My OB-GYN's voice was low and somber, "Your numbers did not double. I need you to come in. Can you be here first thing tomorrow morning?" My heart stopped. "Absolutely."

With a heartfelt response, she told me she was sorry. I looked for a place to sit. My legs were shaking, and my voice quivering as I asked her, "So there's no way, we're not even close?" The doctor voice in her came out then. It was the kind of voice that gets straight to the point while trying to stay human. "It doesn't matter. If the numbers do not at least double, then it's not a viable pregnancy."

I rocked back and forth, gripping the phone tighter and pushing it harder against my ear—as if I wasn't hearing her correctly. I fought my inner voice that wanted to scream at the top of my lungs. Yet, quietly and slowly, I said, "So you're telling me I'm not pregnant?" Her voice changed back to somber. "I'm telling you, your pregnancy is not viable, yes. We need to find out if this is a miscarriage or if this is an ectopic pregnancy."

When I got off the phone, I sat there staring at the wall, trying to wrap my mind around the news. I didn't move. And I don't know how long I sat there not moving and just staring at the wall, but I kept repeating in my head what she had said to me, "It's just not a viable pregnancy."

I hated those words: "not a viable pregnancy," because it was a baby to me. I had already thought about the baby shower and wanted to know if it was a boy or girl. *If it was a girl, what would I name her?* I was already planning my baby's arrival, so to say "viable pregnancy" meant it was nothing. It wasn't anybody. But to me, *there was* a baby inside of me. Regardless of if that baby was not going to live, I felt something growing in me.

When Richard came home, I was at the front door anxiously waiting for him. I spoke so fast; I didn't take a breath. All the while, he did not skip a beat with his normal routine. Boots off, jacket hung, lunch box on the kitchen counter.

He walked past me and didn't say a word. I tried to get a glance at his reaction as I wondered: *why has he not turned around and wrapped his arms around me? Doesn't he have questions, or isn't he wondering if I'm going to be alright?!*

When he finally stopped and looked at me, I took a deep breath; the world seemed to stop. But he coldly said, "What's for dinner?" I ignored his question. "I have a doctor appointment tomorrow morning to go over my options. You are going to come with me, right?"

In response, Richard opened the fridge before saying tersely, "No, I *have* to work. You'll be fine."

I started crying and walked toward him, saying, "I really need you there for me. Are you okay? Do you even care?"

He closed the refrigerator door, looked me square in my eyes, and with no emotion, repeated what my OB-GYN said to me; "It wasn't a viable pregnancy."

I caught myself against the kitchen island, crying so hard I couldn't breathe. In between gasps of air, I asked, *"Are you mad at me?"* As I braced myself for his answer, all I heard were his footsteps walking up the stairs.

The next morning, I got up, drove down the hill, and went to my doctor's appointment. As I was driving down, it felt like the fastest time I'd ever made it to the hospital. I hit every green light. I didn't get behind a slow person. There was no wait when I checked in. My OB-GYN got me in right away.

Everything moved so fast, but I was moving so slow.

The doctor came into the room as I sat on the table with the paper robe on, cold and sad, biting my nails,

"We need to do an ultrasound and find out where we're at with this pregnancy. Where is this egg sitting?" she wondered aloud.

I was agitated that the doctor wouldn't acknowledge this was a baby, not just an egg. I argued with her, *"You mean, we are going to see where my baby is at."*

With a heavy sigh, she tried to explain to me why this wasn't a baby. She gave me the clinical reason.

Angrily, I stopped her mid-sentence, "I felt this human growing."

Before she spoke again, I could see from her face that she was choosing her words carefully. She was processing my body language and increasingly annoyed tone. She delicately said, "You were just feeling nature. You were feeling something growing, but it was never a baby."

I know she was trying to make me feel better about what was going on, but I could tell she was also going through the motions of her job; insert camera in vagina, press on stomach, make "hmm" noises, all the while trying to also give compassion. She used all this medical terminology, and I didn't want it to be used. I wanted this baby to have a name and be treated like a person, but that wasn't the way she wanted to talk about it. She was trying to make me understand...there was never a baby.

I leaned back on the table covered in paper, cold and uncomfortable. As she put the ultrasound device in me, I stiffened up. She gently tapped my knee to relax a bit and forced a smile. We looked at the images on the monitor, and they were a black and white jumbled mess.

My untrained eyes squinted to see if I could make out a human figure; an arm, a leg, any recognizable part. I noticed her eyes focusing on a certain white blob on the monitor. To get a better view, she pushed the uncomfortable instrument up against my right fallopian tube. In her monotone voice, she explained there were no eggs attached in my uterus. I saw her take a quick glance at my face to assess how I was reacting.

She continued, pointing to the monitor, "This is your right fallopian tube." Using the mouse, she circled a small dot. "Here is where your egg has attached." I squinted even harder to try and make out a small dot that looked like it was floating. It was dark gray with nothing around it, almost like a lonely star in a dark night. Yet, as I stared at this dot, my heart knew that dot wasn't supposed to there. It looked out of place. She shifted the camera over to my left side. "For comparison, this is how your fallopian tubes should look like. Clear with no objects inside."

I nodded and turned my head away. I didn't want to see anymore.

When she was done with her examination, I quickly sat up. I was hoping I could clean up and get dressed before we discussed my options. But when she faced me on her chair, I knew I would remain in that paper robe for a little while longer. All I could think about was getting out of the damn thing. It was itchy, and I was sweaty.

Very bluntly, she began, "What we need to do is give you a shot of methotrexate."

I said, "What is that? I've never heard of it."

She said, "It's a cancer drug, and it's going to force your body to release the egg out of your fallopian tubes. You'll bleed a lot. Once that happens, you'll come back in a few days, and we'll do a D&C (dilation and curettage) to remove tissue from inside your uterus."

"Oh, okay."

Even though I knew what I was going there for that morning and that losing the baby was going to happen, I didn't know that I was going to get methotrexate. It felt so wrong, but I knew if I didn't get this done, I couldn't have babies later. I had to have it.

The doctor left the room for a few minutes and returned with a needle filled with the drug. I turned around, leaned forward, and got the shot in my right butt cheek. Afterward, I got dressed and went home.

Once home, I sat in the recliner, crying and mad at myself. I wondered *why did this happen?* I couldn't believe it. Then the methotrexate hit, and it was so painful. I wasn't given anything to lessen the pain, and Tylenol wasn't helping. I had to keep going to the bathroom to see how much blood was coming out.

Then I started seeing chunks of blood come out. From what the doctor had told me, I knew that was the baby—the fertilized egg.

Every time I went to the bathroom and saw evidence of that and the bleeding, I cried so much. Then my husband came home, and I told him what was going on and how much pain I was in. But he just glazed over. Again, I didn't get a hug from him. I didn't get an encouraging word. I didn't get anything. And I couldn't tell if he was mad, sad, or any of his thoughts. I had no idea because he did not talk to me.

Richard went into dinner mode. I couldn't handle it, so I went upstairs to the bedroom and laid there and cried. Then I went to sleep the best I could, but I was up and down all night.

The next morning I got up and ran a bath since I was not bleeding as much. I lie there in the bath, not knowing if I should be taking one. I just wanted to be in the tub because it soothed me.

In the bath, the pain started again. I didn't know if it was because I was moving around a lot or what, but I was having the pain.

Since it was the weekend, I yelled for Richard to please come up and help me out of the tub and into bed. He came upstairs, and I could tell that I was annoying him. Richard sighed and rolled his eyes. He muttered that he was busy with a project as he reluctantly helped me out of the tub and got me dried off.

As we walked from the bathroom to the bed, I hunched over, holding onto him, one arm around my belly, one arm holding onto him. Painfully, I cried out, "Oh my God, this hurts so bad!"

As Richard helped me get into bed, he was forceful and tugged on the blankets hard and quick. He coldly looked at me and said, "You need to get a higher pain threshold."

That was a slap in my face.

This was a man who couldn't even get a splinter out of his finger without me taking him to the emergency room, and *he's telling me I need to get a higher pain threshold?* What an asshole to say that to me.

At this point, I still hadn't heard, "I'm sorry." I hadn't gotten a hug. He hadn't told me he was there for me or that he was mad or sad. I hadn't heard anything.

No, the first thing he said to me was, "You need to get a higher pain threshold."

I don't know why I was shocked because off and on, throughout the years we were together, he constantly put me down and told me that I was just not good enough. When we would argue, and I would stick up for myself, at times, he would get physically abusive.

He would put his hand around my throat or squeeze my head in between his hands and yell at me at the top of his lungs to "Shut the fuck up." He would grab my arms and shove me into the wall. I stayed because I thought, *he's not actually punching me. He's not really abusing me. We're arguing, and he is in the heat of the moment.*

But I always felt like shit about myself.

Him telling me that I needed to get a higher pain threshold made me furious. I thought, *am I the one causing the loss of this baby? It must be my fault. He must blame me because I can't even carry a baby, and we want six kids.*

I got angry at myself for thinking that and in my head, replied, *no, this is my fault because God's saying to me, "You're still in this relationship. I'm not going to let you have a baby, so here is your punishment."*

I went back and forth between being mad at Richard, God, and myself, and from thinking *it's my fault, I can't have a baby, and that's why he's mad at me and hates me* to *why are you thinking this is how he thinks? This is really God's fault because you decided to stay in this relationship.*

Either way, I sliced it, I still blamed myself. It didn't matter that a doctor had told me the pregnancy was a fluke. The chances of it ever happening again were next to zero. Ectopic pregnancies do not happen a lot; they do not have the higher occurrence rate of miscarriages. So I hated myself.

I remember lying back in that bed watching the movie *Love Actually*. I'd wanted to see it when it came out in theaters, but we weren't allowed to go to the movie theater to watch it because it was too much of a rom-com for Richard. Just like we weren't allowed to watch team sports. No football, no hockey, no basketball. I loved basketball and hockey at the time, too.

In our house, we were only allowed to watch individual sports like skateboarding and snowboarding. There was a list of acceptable entertainment to watch, and that movie was not on it.

My husband wasn't going to sit in the room with me and take care of me. He wasn't going to tell me that everything was okay. I watched that movie and cried. I wanted a love like the one they showed in the movie. There wasn't one love story in the movie that captured my soul; it was how, at the end of each love story, the love these couples had for each other gave them happiness. You could see how the characters looked into each other's eyes and felt the love from their partner. I didn't have that love in my marriage.

To this day, that movie is one of my favorites to watch. In the airport scene at the end where they show people coming and going and kissing and hugging, all the families and boyfriends and girlfriends and children...I wanted that. It was not what I was getting at home.

At home, I was told I didn't have a high pain threshold.

A couple of days went by, and again, I said to my husband, "I've got a doctor's appointment. Are you going to come with me?" The answer was the same, "No. Why would I go with you? You know I have to work."

So I took myself down the mountain once more.

Despite pleading with him to come along, he wouldn't go.

Despite my pain, he wouldn't go.

I wasn't in as much pain as I had been on that first drive to the hospital. I tried to think of other things while I was in the car. I listened to music. I let my mind wander and not think about the appointment.

When I got to the hospital, they did an ultrasound. The doctor said, "We're going to have to do a D&C to get everything cleared out and make sure everything's okay."

I didn't realize having a D&C was going to hurt. I understood the concept that it was a vacuum-like procedure. I don't know why I didn't think having a vacuum in my uterus was not going to be a little uncomfortable. *You're vacuuming an organ inside me.* But I didn't think about that.

That machine was so loud, and I could see the suction even though the doctor tried to hide it from me. I thought *there goes the last of my baby.* I just lie there, trying not to show any emotion that it was affecting me as badly as it was. I'm sure she knew it was hard for me since she was a woman. And sadly, she was the only one who hugged me and told me it was okay. I told my parents about it, but my mother and father have never been great at showing emotion with me, so I knew not to expect a hug from them.

After the procedure, the doctor said, "Everything looks good today, but come back in a week or two, for a quick checkup. After that, you can start trying again."

Two weeks later, my bleeding stopped. Richard acted like nothing had happened. My morning routine went back to normal: get up, get dressed, take the dog for a walk, come back, make the dog and myself breakfast, take a shower, go down the hill to either my office or run my household errands to the grocery store and banks, etc. It was all normal again.

Nothing was spoken about in those two weeks before I went

back for my final checkup that I attended by myself. The doctor said, "Everything looks fine. This was probably a big fluke. As soon as you're able, and feel comfortable, feel free to start trying."

A couple of months passed, then my husband and I talked about it, and we did decide to keep on trying.

CHAPTER 2

The Man at the Gas Station

*"Why do you stay in a prison when
the door is wide open?"*
—Anonymous

About a year after I lost the first baby to the ectopic pregnancy, I got pregnant again.

And Richard and I were elated again.

During that time, he still emotionally abused me. Nothing had changed in that department. But I was now separated from my parents and wasn't able to have family time with them. They weren't welcome in my house because my husband and my mother didn't get along. My life revolved solely around him and our business.

When I found out I was pregnant, I was careful and tried not to be so excited. At the same time, I absolutely was. As soon as I found out, I called my doctor, and she immediately prescribed me progesterone pills because of the ectopic pregnancy.

I got my blood drawn again to check my hormone levels. Remember, they wanted to see if my hormones were doubling because if they were, that meant my baby was growing. It's a good sign, and you want them to double. In the first trimester, your baby's forming. Your hormones are nurturing this new human that you're growing, so they have to double every day.

Again, I made the appointment and went down the hill to see my doctor. I went by myself, of course, because my husband was too busy to take the time to drive me and be with me.

At the first appointment, we did a blood draw, and then a couple of days later, I went in for another blood draw.

In that one year, my doctor's business had changed. She had a website, and after the test, I went on there about every five minutes to check my lab results. I refreshed the site, wanting to see what the numbers were. When they finally popped up, I could see that they hadn't doubled, so I turned to Google to try and find out if there was any other research that said they didn't always have to double. But everything I read, every article I saw, in the blogs and forums, no matter what I read, it all said the same thing. Your numbers had to double.

Seeing that my numbers hadn't doubled, I knew that this pregnancy was not going to be a pregnancy.

I just didn't know what was going to happen.

Was this another ectopic pregnancy?

Would it be a miscarriage?

Since I had an appointment for the next day, I talked to the doctor about it. Once again, I was by myself. The doctor said, "You're going to have a miscarriage." Then we did the ultrasound, and she confirmed that the egg had attached to my uterus and not inside my tube.

When I heard the doctor tell me that it was going to be a miscarriage, it was an out of body experience, almost like I was standing behind her looking at myself as I was sitting there on the table with that crummy paper robe freezing.

I was cold and played with my fingernails. As I stared at my hands, I could not believe that this was happening again.

My conversation with the doctor was different this time. She explained that miscarriages are a common occurrence with a lot of women. Many women have them and don't even realize it. They just think they had a really heavy period that month. Or that they were late and then had a heavy period. But, in fact, it was a miscarriage. That did make me feel better a little bit.

On the way home, I cried and asked God, "Do you hate me? I have prayed to you every single night of my entire life; why are you punishing me?"

Even when the doctor told me that this was a cycle of life and a lot of women went through it, I didn't want to hear it. I didn't care if other women had miscarriages. I didn't know these women. They weren't me.

I wanted a baby so badly. Even though I was in an abusive relationship, and we were growing weed illegally, I thought having a baby was going to fix everything. Having a baby would also bring my mom and dad back to my life.

In the car, I kept talking to God. "Why do you hate me? Do you hate me because I'm with him? Do you hate me because we're growing weed? Do you believe it's a gateway drug?" I kept crying and conversating: "He couldn't even come with me. Where are you, God? You're supposed to be here."

It had been ten years since I'd been with my husband at the time.

I questioned myself: *what would I have done differently when I met him at the gas station?*

The first time we saw each other, we didn't even introduce ourselves. I went in to pay for gas, and he gave me a piece of paper and a pen to write my name and number down. After I did, he told me his name. Even though he had the paper in his hand with my number, I introduced myself. He said, "Cool, I'll call you."

That's how I met the guy who would become my husband.

Richard wasn't a man that I normally would go out with. He had long hair, pulled back in a ponytail, and was very rocker-ish with an earring in one ear. He had a motorcycle, and that was the draw for me.

After two or three days, he gave me a call and said, "Hey, this is the guy at the gas station, Richard. Do you remember me?" I nervously answered, *"Yes."* He sounded so different than when I had briefly spoken to him at the gas station. He had this sexy way of talking. Smooth. I could hear him breathing heavily. He continued, "What are you doing tonight? Do you want to go for a ride?" My heart was beating so fast. I was trying to control my voice and sound nonchalant. I always thought men on motorcycles were too cool for me.

There I was, eighteen-years-old with nerdy glasses; I never wore makeup and had the fashion sense of an iguana. Even though I was trying to play it cool, my answer came out too fast, "Absolutely." I gave him my address, and we went for a ride, had some dinner, and didn't separate. From that day on, we were rarely apart for eighteen years.

On my way home after losing my second child, I thought, *why didn't I just walk away? Why did I even stick with this man?* I asked God, "If I got divorced, would you allow me to find somebody else in my life to have a child with?"

But as I said the words sitting in the car, making the long drive up the hill once more, I knew I'd made a commitment to Richard. I needed to stay loyal, and I didn't want to give up.

Part of me felt like ours was a normal relationship, and that part had to do with what I had gone through in my childhood.

Growing up, my mother was very hard on me and always said negative things to me. I was always too fat; my grades were never good enough (even though I got As); I was never pretty enough. So hearing those same words from Richard was normal.

Even though my reality wasn't normal.

I knew when we argued, and he choked me or grabbed my arm so hard that he would leave bruises, that it wasn't normal. I knew when he grabbed my face and yelled at me as loud as he could, as close to my face as he could; it wasn't right.

But I would blame myself for the argument: if I didn't talk back, if I wasn't so argumentative, then it wouldn't have happened. I wouldn't have pushed him to it.

On my drive home, I asked God, "Is it because I'm this way? Are you trying to tell me something different? Aren't I supposed to stay because aren't I supposed to be loyal? I'm not supposed to run away, right?"

Besides, leaving seemed too easy. I had to stick it out because I'd sworn I would be there for better or for worse.

At the appointment, the doctor had asked me if I wanted to do another D&C, and I said no. I wanted to see if my body would expel the baby naturally. I didn't want to go through feeling a vacuum enter me again, and I didn't want to hear that noise. When I told her that, she said, "Okay, it will start happening in a couple of days, but if you feel like you want to come in to get double checked, just let me know. We'll get you right in."

The next couple of days, I was beyond in tune with my body. I could feel everything. I was hyper-aware of every sensation. Each little twinge, twist, and ping sent me to the bathroom wondering, *is it starting now?* Since I'd always had bad, heavy periods that would last a week, I knew what to expect with normal bleeding. But I didn't know what to expect with a miscarriage.

When I started bleeding, it was exceptionally heavy. I let it happen naturally and bled for over seven days. I wrapped my head around the fact that I was having a miscarriage and accepted that it was natural. In my mind, I reasoned, *now I've had an ectopic pregnancy and a miscarriage. Nothing else could possibly go wrong.*

I do remember a moment when I was talking to my sister-in-law, telling her about what had happened. She replied, "You know, Toni, this is probably going to sound harsh, but if it's not meant to be right now, it's not meant to be." That really hurt my feelings because this was a girl who had her own beautiful little girl. She and her husband hadn't tried. Their pregnancy had been an accident. She was young and had suffered no complications. Then she'd had a perfect child.

Instead of saying, "You know what, that hurt," I kept my retort inside." I should have said to her then, "You have this beautiful girl, and I just had a miscarriage, and that's what you say to me?" But I felt like I would be a bad person if I shared that what she said hurt my feelings. All because *it's a natural thing and happens to a lot of women.* All because I told myself, *I can't feel sorry for myself for having a baby and having this miscarriage.*

So I kept my feelings inside, went about my day, and I soon recovered. But I did stop praying. Every night because I was so angry, I pushed my feelings deeper and deeper inside me.

CHAPTER 3

You Can Go Now

*"It was a shameful thing that she had
nothing of which to be ashamed."*
–Philip José Farmer

After the miscarriage, I thought we should talk to an IVF doctor to see if there were tests out there I didn't know about to determine if I would have trouble conceiving. I figured *there might be something that my normal doctor isn't seeing in these tests.* And I definitely did not want to go through losing any more babies. So Richard and I sought a second opinion.

I Googled a whole bunch of the best IVF doctors within my area and checked out how long they had practiced, why they got into IVF, what their results were, and the percentage of their live births. After a little digging, I discovered that some doctors added viable pregnancies to their live birth percentages even though the woman may not have carried to term and lost the baby. In the percentage of live births, they would call the baby a "baby" as long as it went past the first trimester. Since I saw these fluffed numbers, I wanted to make sure I found a doctor, who, when they referred to a live birth, meant the woman had carried the baby to full-term and given birth. I didn't want the percentages to include a lady who was able to keep an egg fertilized past the first trimester.

In addition to Googling, I also went on a couple of IVF forums to see what people were saying about certain doctors. I asked a few questions there and then finally settled on a doctor in downtown Sacramento who had been doing IVF for quite some time.

After I made the appointment, I begged my husband to come with me. I pleaded, "Please, just one time come with." I heard the same excuse as before: he had too much to do. Then he asked me, "Why would I go? I'm just going to be sitting there while you're answering questions. Your doctor's saying everything should be fine. I think this is a waste of money, but if you want to go, go."

Everything was about money with him. Since we didn't have health insurance, we were paying out of pocket for health care. But in the eleven years that we had been together by then, we had discussed that we wanted a big family. I wanted at least two kids. By then, I would have been happy with one. Still, we had always talked about having six kids. And I was struggling to have one.

I kept saying to him, "But don't you want to have a family, too? Because if you don't want to have a family, just tell me. But if you want to have a family, and this has happened to us twice now, don't you want to go and see what this doctor says? Don't you want to know about the tests that you have to do, too?"

He simply said, "Eh, I know I'm fine."

But I pressed him. "How do you know that? You don't have kids. You've never had a kid."

In that moment, he had already placed blame on me. It was one of the first times he'd remarked that he did blame me.

I accepted his little jabs of me not being good enough because I'd heard them all my life. When it comes to my mother and father, I realize they love me. I am their child, but they are very non-emotional. There's never been a time in my life where my mother and father have told me they love me. There's never been a time in my life where my mother has hugged me. She's never told me she's proud of me. She's never been emotionally supportive.

Listening to Richard blame me wasn't that different than receiving the non-emotional treatment I was used to. I accepted the fact that he wasn't going to go with me to the IVF appointment. I had to go to that appointment alone, and I was so embarrassed when I walked into that office.

In the waiting, couples room sat together. I saw a lesbian couple being there for each other. Every single person had someone, and I walked in without anyone.

As soon as I was in the door, all eyes were on me. People looked at me with such sadness, like they were saying, "Wow, we feel bad for you."

When I got to the front desk, the lady behind the counter handed me a clipboard and said, "Here's the paperwork you need to fill out." Then she peered behind me and asked, "Is your significant other parking the car, or are they going to be right here? Are they running a little bit late?"

With my shoulders hunched and my voice low, so no one in the room would hear me, I said, "No, I'm here by myself."

Then she asked me, "Will you be doing this with a partner,

or are you going to be doing IVF alone?" Meaning, was I going to be buying a stranger's sperm? Everyone in the waiting room could hear what she was asking me. We were not in a room by ourselves having a private conversation.

Trying to sound strong, I looked up at her and replied, "No, I have a partner. He's just not here. He could not come with me today." She confirmed that my husband was a male.

Then she said, "Well, answer his side of the questions as best you can because typically your significant other should be here with you." *Could I get anymore punches in the gut?* The wind was knocked out of me.

When I turned back to find a seat, I tried not to make eye contact with any of the couples. I found an empty seat in the very back corner away from everyone, where I kept my head down, crossed my legs, and filled out the paperwork. But I was nervous. I felt sorry for myself. I was so embarrassed. My feet swung back and forth as I tried to the best of my ability to answer all the questions.

There were a lot of questions, questions about how many sexual partners had I had? How many sexual partners had he had? Had I been pregnant before? If so, give details about the pregnancy. Why do we want a baby?

On his side, it was, "How many times do you masturbate?" "Do you do drugs?" "What kind of drugs?" "Do you drink?" "How many times do you drink during the week?" "Do you smoke?"

I answered everything I could and handed in my clipboard, then returned to my seat to wait to be called back to the exam room.

When they called my name, the nurse led me back to the exam room, where I met with the doctor. Again, I was asked: "Is your significant other with you today?"

Once more, I said, "No," he's not. He had to work."

The doctor took a moment to gather his thoughts. I could tell he wanted to be delicate yet firm in his next question to me. He was an older doctor who had years of untold knowledge. His tired gray eyes were stern yet concerned when he asked, "Is he as serious as you are to have this baby? Because IVF is a very emotional rollercoaster. It takes a lot out of you as a female because of all the tests we're going to be doing. There are a lot of classes you have to take. Is he going to be there to support you?" He paused and looked at me for a long moment before saying, "This is a big commitment. If we decide to take you in as a patient, we're going to be together for a lot of months. Is he definitely committed?"

I said, "Yeah, he just had a lot of meetings today. He couldn't come." He slowly nodded and breathed a huge sigh. As he looked back down at my paperwork, his shoulders slumped in disappointment. The doctor was not satisfied with my answer, but he left it alone.

I felt ashamed. I had let this man down who I had just met a few minutes ago. His eyes asked the same questions I asked Richard when I needed him to explain himself, "If it was that important, he couldn't move his meetings around?" Or, "You couldn't have made this appointment when he didn't have meetings?" I couldn't answer the questions I knew the doctor was thinking. I didn't know the real reason my husband wasn't there.

He studied my history and medical chart, and I picked at my nails and read his "Best Dad" coffee mug twelve times. I peered at the photos of all the babies he had helped bring into the world, twenty-eight times. I squinted my eyes and envisioned a picture of my future family and me on his wall. After the shuffling of my medical chart stopped, he sighed heavily and said, "I'm going to be really honest with you, Toni. Probably the biggest issue is that you're fat."

When I heard those words, I flashed back to my husband, telling me that it was all my fault that I couldn't have a baby. Now, this doctor was telling me it was my fault because I couldn't keep my BMI score at a healthy level.

By no means did I feel like I was fat. I exercised regularly. I ate fairly decently, but on a BMI chart, I was considered obese. When the doctor told me I was fat, that was it. I knew everything was all my fault. Immediately, I thought, *God, why are you punishing me?*

Then I was mad at myself. I was mad at Richard for not being there for me. While I was told I was fat, and it was all my fault, my husband should have been sitting there next to me, holding my hand.

As I left, I thought, *why can't I just be a better person? Why don't I know what He wants me to be?*

Driving home, I was upset that my husband wasn't there. At the same time, I was not upset because if he had been there, he would've heard the doctor call me fat. If he would've heard what the doctor had said, then he would've used it against me later. Then he could say once more that everything we had been through was my fault.

I never felt fat and ugly when I was with my husband because he had never said that I was ugly. He always said that I was beautiful. I only felt fat and ugly when I saw my mother. She would tell me that I needed to lose more weight or ask, "Why did you cut your hair that way?" Or, "Why are you putting your makeup on like that?" She always badgered me about my looks.

I didn't know if her doing that was a cultural thing.

Although, I understood that a lot of daughters in Asian families felt the same way about how their mothers treated them. But the one thing I had going for me was that my husband had never made me feel like I was not beautiful. Then I heard that doctor, and while I might not have felt fat because my husband never said those words, it made me feel like in addition to my husband telling me it was my fault, now the doctor was adding proof to that accusation. I was fat in the doctor's estimation, and it was now more my fault than my husband's.

My doctor came up with a game plan to get me to lose weight. First, I had to get my hormone levels checked. Next, I had to be very precise in knowing when my period was to start and when it would end. I needed this knowledge because two weeks before my period, I had to go into the doctor's office to get a blood test and check my hormone levels. Then two days before my period was to start; I would get my hormone levels checked again to see if my body had produced enough eggs.

I also had to do an x-ray test that used a dye, but it could only be done when I was on my period. And I had to take it on the heaviest day.

On that day, I had to go into the x-ray room where numerous people were present. It was not just a single person like you might encounter when you get your ankle or finger x-rayed. About four or five different people were in the x-ray room, both male and female. I was on my period, bleeding heavily, and lying there naked. No tampon. No pad. Just on a sheet of paper, bleeding.

I felt so vulnerable sitting there with all those people around me. Although I knew that medical professionals performed this test on a regular basis, it still didn't make me feel any better.

As I lie there, they took a tube of dye and put it in me. Then they released the dye and took a series of x-rays. It wasn't painful. But I felt the tube go in and the dye release and travel through my body.

They use the dye to see if you have any blockage in your tubes. I lie there for about thirty minutes, bleeding everywhere, and when I was done, they gave me one of those blue sheets to clean myself up with. So the embarrassment continued since I was in the room trying to wipe and clean myself. They gave me a big pad to put on. When I walked out of the room, I couldn't stop staring at the floor to avoid the eyes of the lady who had checked me in. Studying the tile, I said, "Can I go now?"

She said, "Yeah, go ahead."

So, I got out of there as fast as possible.

I could not get home soon enough.

After a week, the results came back, and the doctor said everything was fine. I had a little bit of endometriosis (a disease where the tissue that is supposed to grow inside your uterus grows outside of it), but I could still get pregnant. It wouldn't affect anything. Still, the doctor wanted to put me on hormone pills and have me do injections.

My issue never was that my body couldn't produce a normal amount of eggs. But the injections were meant to increase egg production. The hormones were to support it. Regardless, this was what I was to do. The first week before my period would start, I would start taking progesterone pills, and then I would give myself hormone injections to increase my body's production of eggs. The day before ovulation, I had to give myself a big injection to make my eggs drop.

All of these injections meant that Richard and I had to take some classes on how to give yourself injections. My husband had to be there. There was no way around it. It was mandatory.

Despite this, I had to beg him to go to these classes for weeks. Because the class was done at 8:00 pm, he couldn't use the "I have to work today" excuse. We didn't play or watch sports, and our friends and business partners would be home with their families at that time. So there was no reason for him not to go other than the fact it was an inconvenience for him to get showered, dressed, and drive down the hill with me.

The place where we were to take classes was about an hour's drive away one-way, meaning we would be on the road two hours total. My husband argued, "By the time we get home, it's going to be 11:00," and, "I don't understand why we need to do this." But I begged him, and begged him, and begged him. I kept saying, "This is going to help us have a baby. And the chances of us having twins goes up because what if more than one egg drops?" He finally said he'd go. I thought when Richard agreed to go; I would be excited. Yet, I felt anger.

I was the one seeing the OB-GYN and the infertility doctor on my own. I was taking left and right jabs on every aspect of having a baby. OUR baby. And instead of supporting me, Richard fought me every step of the way! He'd told me he wanted a family. So, why was he not supporting me?

Is Richard blaming me because he is not a father yet? Is he thinking this is all pointless? Is he regretting marrying me because I am less of a woman and can't bear children? All these questions kept running through my mind. They were all the questions he refused to answer.

We did make it to the classes where they taught you how to inject yourself. I could do the injection on myself in different spots on my body. We got a little orange, and the instructors gave us some needles to practice with. But the one big injection to release the eggs had to be given by him, in my bum. This injection required a big needle and for him to learn how to make a stabbing motion, which would require just one stab in my butt.

After we completed the classes, I got the syringes. Then, the day came where I needed to start the shots. A week before I began ovulating, I gave myself injections every single day. It was not the easiest thing to stick a needle in myself every day, but I was bound and determined to make it happen.

Not only was I injecting myself and planning on having Richard inject me, but I had changed my diet to vegan. I was exercising. I was doing everything I needed to make sure that I had a healthy baby.

Then it was his turn.

The day came for my husband to give me the big injection so I could release my eggs. He threw a fit as we stood there, and I waited for him to give it to me, as he said, "I can't believe I have to do this. This is going to be so horrible. I can't believe you're making me put this injection in you. I can't do this. I can't stick this in you. What are you even doing this for?"

As I stood in the middle of our bathroom, bent over the sink with my pants down, my head spun. As Richard paced back and forth, yelling over and over the same line, "I can't do this; why are we doing this," I got scared. Usually, when Richard yelled like that, it meant I was going to get slapped. And as he got more and more agitated, I felt more and more vulnerable, leaning over the sink.

After ten minutes of battling with him to "Just do it...just do it...it's not going to hurt." I pleaded, "We've talked about this before, and I've marked my skin with a Sharpie. So, just do it. You could've been done by now." But the whole time, he never stopped talking about what it was doing to him to be put in the situation and how difficult it was.

I thought to myself; *this is difficult for you? Dude, I've been injecting myself for a week. I've lost a baby to a miscarriage by myself. I had to have a D&C by myself. I got methotrexate injected into me and lost our baby by myself. You can put this needle in my butt.*

He finally gave me the shot.

Six weeks later, I was pregnant for the third time.

CHAPTER 4

God, Are You Serious?

"I've lost count of the times
He (God) let me down."
—Denis Law

The experience with my third pregnancy was a little different.

After the IVF and the injection, I was automatically scheduled for an appointment to come in and start doing blood tests to determine if I was pregnant. Taking a urine test when you're on progesterone is pretty much going to give a false positive, so the doctor advised me to stay away from those kinds of tests.

As all of this was going on, I felt confident. I just knew: *this is going to go absolutely right.* And it did. My numbers *did* start going up. I was ecstatic but cautious. Every time I got blood drawn for my HCG numbers, I constantly searched on the doctor's website, looking for my hormone numbers to double. When I did see them double, I gave myself a high five, reinforcing my belief that *I'm being very cautious.*

And I stayed cautious.

I was on partial bed rest and limited activity right from the get-go and really took it easy, but my husband was not home much. He stayed away from me. I don't know to this day whether he was doing that to ease my stress or if he was choosing not to be home. But he wasn't home a lot. He wasn't telling me whether he was excited or worried about what was going on. There was no communication between us. It was simply me doing the pregnancy on my own.

I kept going to get my blood work done. The numbers kept going up. Then one day, I felt a little shoulder pain. I don't remember what I was doing. All I know was that I was home. I don't know if I was in the kitchen, in the shower, or lying in bed. I just remember that I was home and sensing pain in my right shoulder.

I recalled thinking, *oh no, oh no...but wait, maybe my right arm sort of hurts*, too, *not just my shoulder*. I had to go in the next day anyway to get my numbers done.

At the appointment, I hastily told the nurse at the reception desk that I had pain in my right shoulder and gave her a quick rundown of my history. After looking over my latest test results, the nurse commented, "Your numbers have been going up. They're doubling. But let's go ahead and double-check. We'll do an ultrasound today. It might be a little bit too early to see, but let's check where we're at."

Nervously, I got undressed and on the table.

I don't know why doctors' offices can't give you a better option than those little paper robes to wear. I put on the stinky thing anyway and lie back down.

When the ultrasound wand goes inside you, it's uncomfortable *every single time*. The nurse, whom I had never met, looked around my uterus. I watched her facial expressions carefully. It was becoming easier to tell when doctors and nurses were about to give me bad news. Their eyes dropped down to their hands; their lips drew to a point. This nurse's expressions were no different. She stared at the screen a little harder. We both squinted at the monitor.

Then she moved the device toward one of my tubes, and all of a sudden, we both saw the little gray spot. She turned to me and said, "It's an ectopic pregnancy, Toni. I'm sorry."

As I studied her face, I could see she was almost as let down as I was. I could tell the difference in her expression between the time I had told her about the right shoulder pain and now. Before she saw that little dot, she looked confident and said, "Your numbers are going good. They're doubling." I had seen in her expression that she felt like I was being a little too cautious with every little pain I felt. That because I was so in tune with my body, it was almost freaking me out. But I *could* feel every heartbeat and my blood coursing through my veins.

When she saw it was an ectopic pregnancy, I saw the disappointment on her face.

Then I got silent.

She left the room. I cleaned up, got dressed, and waited for her to come back. But I already knew what was going to happen.

She was getting the methotrexate to inject me. Then I would come back after a few more days, have the D&C, and it would be back to dealing with now the loss of a third child.

I was more devastated from the loss of this pregnancy than the other two because I'd done everything I was supposed to do. I was eating healthy. I was exercising regularly. I wasn't drinking. I'd stopped smoking weed. I was trying my best to keep stress at bay. I did whatever I needed to do. Everything that I was told to do to have a healthy baby, I'd made sure I did it. There were no sodas, no Gatorades, no sugar, no nothing. Everything I wanted to eat, I didn't. Every recommendation the fertility doctor had given me, I had done to a T.

Before I'd left for that appointment, I hadn't told my husband about the pain in my shoulder. I'd just said I was leaving for a doctor's appointment. Then I went to my doctor's appointment alone because *what was the point of asking Richard to come with me?* I knew his answer was going to be no.

So I went down the hill by myself for an innumerable time only to find out it was another ectopic pregnancy.

All the way home, on top of blaming myself for losing this baby, I thought, *how am I going to tell Richard so I can make it less painful for him?* Here was a man who couldn't even go to doctors' appointments with me, yet I was worried about how this was going to affect *him?*

Meanwhile, in the back of my head, I was also blaming God. I said, *God, are you serious? There are women out there who kill their babies, who beat them to death, who drown them, who neglect them, who don't feed them. You gave them babies, and you can't give me one? I'm that bad of a person that I can't get one?*

Instead of delving deeper into my feelings about losing another child, I pushed them aside to think about how to tell a man who couldn't drive me and sit with me at a clinic with my doctor who had just told me we were losing our third baby. My brain echoed, *how is this going to affect him?*

The first couple of times that I'd told Richard we were losing our baby, he'd given me no reaction, so I don't know what I was expecting the third time. I was half expecting he would finally give me a hug and tell me it was going to be okay. I hoped he would at last say, "You know what? I'm going to start being there for you." I wanted him to hold me when I cried. This was the movie rolling through my head just like *Love Actually*. I wanted that love so bad, but there I was driving home wondering *how am I going to tell him?*

When I drove up the driveway, I could see Richard outside with his friends. They were smoking a joint and laughing, and he was cracking jokes like he was a stand-up comedian. Anger stormed my body. *This asshole can find time to hang out with friends, yet he can't hold his wife's hand while losing HIS baby?!!* I raced up to my bedroom and crashed into bed, bawling so hard my face hurt, crumbling inside.

I had been so worried about HIS feelings, yet he couldn't care less about mine! He must've heard the front door shut because I caught a glimpse of him looking back at me as I stomped upstairs. As I lie there holding onto my pillow, shedding more tears than I have ever shed, I hoped Richard would come into our room. I had an image in my mind that he would lie next to me and scoop me up so tight that I could feel his heartbeat with mine. Instead, I heard the bedroom door swing open, "What the F*&K? Are you seriously that rude?" There was no mention of my doctor appointment. No question of how I was holding up. Nothing. Once again, I was less than dirt on his boot.

Because this pregnancy had gone into the second trimester, there was concern that damage to one of my tubes had occurred. To determine if there was damage, I had to do the dye contrast x-ray that I had done previously when I was menstruating.

Since I'd had two ectopic pregnancies and a miscarriage, having children was going to be difficult for me. Two ectopic pregnancies forming is not a normal biological thing that happens in a woman. Something was preventing my egg from going to where it needed to go to become a fertilized egg in my uterus. The doctors didn't know what it was, and that meant another dye test.

I'd also been told that if I kept on trying to have babies, the risk for ectopic pregnancies was high. I could have another one. And there might not be any more babies. Period. I might be so damaged that I could never have a baby at all.

Those were the thoughts I'd had while driving home by myself and wondering how to tell my husband—as if he was going to care.

On the day of my appointment, the doctor told me, "We don't see any blockage. We can't explain why this is happening. We just can't. The amount of endometriosis you have is very minimal. You don't show any other problems with the uterus. We just don't know. But we do know that you can't have another ectopic pregnancy again and that your risk of having a miscarriage is very high."

But I still wanted to keep trying.

I keep thinking *there's no way God's going to let this happen a fourth time.*

*"You can't hurt someone you love…
and that's how I now know you
truly never loved me."*
–Jarod Kintz

After my third pregnancy, Richard and I kept on trying, even though I knew it was going to be a risk.

I almost didn't care.

My mission was just to have a baby.

I thought having a child would give me the fulfilling life that I wanted so badly. Friends around me had the Norman Rockwell family life with loved ones around for the holidays and running kids to preschool, soccer, or whatever families do. I wanted that lifestyle. I wanted that love they looked like they had—and that I was missing.

My days consisted of trying to make everybody else happy. I went through the motions of everyday life, knowing there was more for me out there. But every time I tried to lift myself up and improve my career as a Realtor; a career I loved; I'd get pushed back down by my husband.

When I got pregnant the fourth time, I hoped it was going to happen. Before I knew that my fourth pregnancy was an ectopic pregnancy, I had told myself *there's just no way that this can happen again*. I reasoned *it's just me feeling the pain in my right shoulder. There's no way God's going to make that happen a fourth time with a fourth baby and a third ectopic pregnancy. No way*. Besides, I asked myself, *how can one woman have so much bad luck?*

But I was in pain. Even though I argued with myself.

In the back of my head, I just kept thinking; *I have to get a higher pain threshold*.

My mind raced back to the moment when my husband first spoke those words to me.

When we would fight through the years, I would bring up in the argument that he had said that to me, telling him, "You remember when you said I needed to get a higher pain threshold? Well, I want out. I want a divorce."

Yet, even as I said those words, I felt a loyalty to him. Marriage vows meant never leaving.

In the midst of such an unhealthy relationship, I was trying to have a baby with him, thinking everything was going to change, and it'd make me happy. I don't know if I thought this way because I just wanted someone to love me, but I really wanted to be a mother.

I wanted to have a child, so I could be loving to that child, so that child would always know that his or her mom was going to be there. I was going to have open arms and would constantly tell it, "I love you." All the things I never had, that child was going to have. I wanted to give a human being that feeling I had wanted my whole life.

Life went on.

Then one night, I got up to make dinner, and for the first time, my husband, who rarely ever showed any nurturing behavior toward me, saw how white my face got. I was in so much pain, and he could see it all over me; I couldn't speak and tell him that we needed to go to the hospital. He just read my face and asked me if I was okay. I didn't say a word but blankly looked at him as he said, "Get in the truck. We're going to the emergency room." I didn't fight him. I just went right along with what he said. I was a little shocked, but at the same time was in a lot of pain. As we drove, I wanted to stay stoically fierce.

Once we got to the emergency room, they immediately took me in, did an ultrasound, took some blood, and then noted that my blood pressure was low. During the ultrasound, they could see that I had allowed my ectopic pregnancy to go so long that my right tube was splitting. I was internally bleeding and had been for some time.

Doctors immediately scheduled me for surgery. But it was a busy night. They didn't have any rooms. They were waiting for the on-call OB-GYN surgeon to come in while I sat in a hallway on a gurney because they didn't have any rooms. They monitored me for hours on a morphine drip. Finally, the doctor arrived. She grabbed my hand and said, "Are you ready?"

I grabbed her hand right back and asked, "Are *you* ready? Did you get enough sleep?" I was petrified but trying not to show it. I'd read stories about how doctors don't ever get enough sleep, and they make mistakes. So I was scared that I was going to be one of those statistics. She told me, "I'm fine. I've gotten plenty of sleep. I'm ready, are you ready?"

I told her, "Just take both the tubes out. Just stop it."

And she said, "I can't. I'm only going to take the one that needs to be out. I'm not going to let you make this decision when you're this distraught. We're doing one. If I need to take the left one because there's a lot of intricate damage, then I'll make that decision. But I'm not going to let you voluntarily take it out."

For the first time in ten years, my mother and father saw my husband when they all gathered in the emergency room. It was also the first time that my parents had come down during any of my pregnancies and losses. They were supportive of me having the tube removed and going into emergency surgery. And I wasn't there to see their reactions in the emergency room and what they said to each other. I just remember that I was in the surgical room for a lot longer than they thought I would be. Another family was in the emergency room as well, and a pastor came in to talk to them because their family member had passed away.

But that pastor had mistaken my family as the one that he needed to talk to. So when he came up and introduced who he was, apparently my mother was crushed. After the mistake was cleared up and the pastor had apologized, he went to the other family. My parents were relieved, and so was my ex-husband. And I don't know if that was an eye-opener for them or what, but after over a decade of not speaking a word to Richard, they started talking to him.

My parents didn't see my ex-husband too many times after that incident, but I could at least talk to my mother about him. I felt more comfortable going to visit them more, and I could see that my mother really did love me. Maybe I was mistaking her non-emotional personality trait as something more that I just didn't understand. All I know was, I learned she was there because she cared.

After the surgery, I found out that I had lost my right tube, which was the better of the two. Now, I couldn't have babies ever, and I was devastated. There I was in my thirties and married. Society expects that you are supposed to be a mother by then. You're not supposed to *not* have children.

Instead of dealing with the pain, I went through life. I didn't think about how I'd almost died. If I would not have gone to the emergency room, if my husband hadn't noticed how much pain my face must have shown and taken it seriously, I would have died. My tube would have burst within 24-48 hours, and I would have bled out because there was no way I would have made it to the hospital in time. I lived too far from the hospital, way up in the mountains. I would have let myself die to have a child that wasn't going to happen.

In the aftermath of the fourth loss, I battled my mind, not wanting to accept that I was not good enough. But I was in denial because I hated myself. I hated myself for not being able to have one of the things I most yearned for in life.

That led to drinking and doing cocaine. I went back to smoking a lot of weed and ingesting whatever it took for me to not think about losing those babies. I was spiraling, and even though I knew a lot of why I was out of control, I still wasn't accepting of the fact that my whole life was a lie. Everybody on the outside looking in thought we were this happy, loving couple and that Richard was a doting husband to me.

Richard had a pet name for me that he called me all the time, "Precious." I hated it. Still, he rarely called me by my name. The few times he did, my own name didn't even sound right anymore. Women would hear Richard call out, "Precious," and would tell me how lucky I was to have a husband who wasn't ashamed to call me such a sweet name. In public, we looked like we had nothing but love for each other. But we were #relationshipgoals, not real goals.

Behind the scenes, it wasn't good. Everyone thought I was moving on okay, that he was being so emotionally supportive when the whole time it was the complete opposite. I was living a lie and not admitting what was going on. And not having anybody to talk to was killing me. Add to that the fact that I hated myself.

I let myself go. I didn't put on makeup. I told myself every day that I was fat and ugly. That I couldn't make anybody happy and was not doing enough in my life. I repeated to myself that I was not living up to God, and He was not showing me the way I needed to go. He was not lifting me. I asked myself: *where are my footprints in the sand?*

Then I stopped doing IVF.

There was no point. My thought process was *if it happens, it happens, but it probably won't because it hasn't happened yet.*

I continued on with my life, scared that one day we would get busted for illegally growing weed, and my life would be ruined.

But I disappoint everybody in my life anyway, so who cares?

I didn't want to foster children, and I didn't want to adopt. That part of me felt selfish and like a little bitch. I could have a family, and I knew that since there are so many kids out there who need one. I could be that person, but I didn't think that I could love somebody else's child who wasn't biologically mine.

At the same time, I hated the fact that a woman could give birth to a child at all. And I was mad that God had allowed that woman (any woman) to give birth to a child who she didn't want for whatever reason. How ironic was that? I wanted a child. I was mad at God for not giving me one when I could easily have adopted a child or fostered a child and changed that child's life for the better. But I was so hateful about how that child got into foster care that I didn't want to do it.

Right after losing our fourth child, my mom saw an *Oprah* episode about how you could pay a woman in India to be your surrogate. One village was full of Indian women who were surrogates to American moms, and she said, "Why don't you look into doing that?" But I didn't want that. I wanted to carry a baby. I wanted to have that feeling and was downright jealous that these women could do it because my eggs were fine. My body had producing ovaries, just like every other woman who could give birth. The problem was getting the egg out of the tube and into where it needed to go.

When I told my mom how I felt about the surrogacy, her response was, "I'm giving you an option to have a kid. It's cheaper than having a surrogate here in the states. You can use one in India, but if you don't want to, you must not really want one."

Must not really want one? What do you think I've tried to do these last four times I was pregnant? Why would I try if I didn't really want one? How dare you say that to me! On top of that, where am I going to get the money? I've spent thousands of dollars on IVF. And spending money when you're dealing drugs and growing weed illegally is not the easiest thing to do. We have something called the IRS. What do you expect me to do?

I was so pissed off at what she said that when I got home, I went on a cocaine binge for two days.

Life continued.

The sun still set.

The sun still rose.

The days still went.

Life doesn't care what you're going through; it still moves ahead.

Before long, my husband and I decided to sell the house that we had built ourselves. We moved into another house to appease his grandparents.

We closed one chapter and entered another.

CHAPTER 6

You Will Not Believe This

"Your worst enemy could be your best friend
and your best friend, your worst enemy."
–Bob Marley

Early on in our relationship, Richard's grandma passed away. Then his grandfather remarried another, much younger lady. They moved away but eventually came back. When they did, my husband wanted them to be a part of our lives. His grandfather was basically his father.

When I say Richard was the youngest of thirteen, I mean his grandfather treated him like he was his son, and his aunts and uncles treated him like he was their sibling. That's why he was always called the youngest of thirteen. Everyone was pretty close, which was attractive to him and why he wanted a large family.

Contrast that with my life, my two parents and one uncle (more like my older brother), who my father adopted and brought to the states when he was in the military, and that was the only family I had.

My grandfather on my father's side loved me, but I didn't get to see him a lot because my father was in the military. When I did get to see him, he doted and loved on me. My grandmother, however, was indifferent.

I don't know if it was because my father was the first one in our family to marry outside of his race, but my grandmother definitely treated me differently. Everybody in the family felt it and knew it. So, I didn't feel any connection with her.

When we left the Philippines to come to the United States, I had only met my grandfather on my mother's side a couple of times, and that was it. That left just the three people on my side of the family: my parents and my uncle.

When my husband's side of his huge family had these big get-togethers, I loved it. I wanted that, too. So, that was the draw for wanting a close-knit family.

It made it easy to move when we learned his grandparents needed a place to move into. We wanted to be closer and planned to sell the house that we'd spent a couple of years building ourselves. We would buy a place twenty minutes closer to town, with some acreage, and then build his grandparents a house.

I was devastated to leave my house. When we sold it, oh, how I cried. I remember standing there in the street on the last day we were there, bawling. The neighbor came over and hugged me. He was such a nice guy and said, "It's sad to see you guys leave. I understand that this must be really hard, but off to better and greater things."

I was sad, also because that chapter of living in that house carried so much meaning. I'd lost four kids in that house. The memory of everything that had happened was all in that house.

Now, I can look back today and see myself standing on that street. I can see the house through my eyes, and I'm crying. Not only because I really loved that house, but because a lot of sweat equity and love went into it. It was my first house. And of course, I was crying for that reason, but I was also sad because I felt I would never be able to revisit that part of my story again.

I now know I wasn't just crying because I was leaving the house; I was crying because I was leaving a memory. I was walking away from a very important part of my life, and I hadn't dealt with any of the memories.

I also know I get attached to things. Physical items to me bring a memory and touch me. They make me remember. On the day we left, I watched *Love Actually* again. It sounds so silly and minute, but when I think about it today, as I walked away from that house, that was one of my memories. That movie touched me at a moment when I needed something to.

Leaving that house was hard. I also was reluctant to do it based on what my husband's grandfather wanted. I wanted to help him and his wife, but at the same time, I didn't.

Prior to selling the house, Richard and I originally had purchased an acre of land right down the street where we were building a house for his grandparents. Then Richard decided, without discussing his intentions with me, that his grandparents and the two of us should be on one property (that was the acreage we'd bought twenty minutes away) versus building them a house down the street.

I had no control over my life. No control over any decisions. My husband made every decision of our life without me. He was in charge of every aspect of what we did, including the money part. I was limited on how much I could work as a Realtor, and when I would make any commissions, it had to go to the household. Any decision didn't include me.

We bought the new property and started building our house. Somehow or another, the grandparents started fighting. They were frustrated because as we were building our house, they were living in their RV plugged into our house.

Confined quarters are rough. They didn't have any separation and didn't feel comfortable coming into our house because of our need for privacy. So they argued more and more until they decided to get a divorce. Then the step-grandma became angrier and angrier at us because she thought we weren't building their house fast enough.

But we had all these delays, and it didn't really matter what they were. The step-grandma could see that no one was at fault for the delays, but she didn't want to accept it.

And while we were trying to build their house, we were also trying to give the grandfather a hobby, so he would not just sit in the RV. He'd always wanted a horse, so when we bought the property, we made sure we had room for a horse and built a barn. Remember, we were building this all on our own because it was a lot cheaper than having someone else do it for us. Plus, we were trying to build our house and manage our illegal weed operation while not getting into trouble.

I got lost in the whole situation, trying to make everybody around me happy again. Trying to make Richard happy. Trying to make our friends happy—who were over at our house every single day. Every aspect of my life had to do with them. There was nothing for me anymore. It was all, "You have to do this. You have to do that."

When the step-grandma filed for divorce, things got messier. In California, if you file for divorce and are living with your grandchild, you are allowed to sue for palimony. So the step-grandma sued us, and it was legal. She didn't tell us that she was going to sue us. She didn't say a word even though she was still living on our property and threatening to call the authorities and throw us in jail. She didn't care that Richard and I were paying all her bills. I had to find out what she was doing from a fax that a lawyer had sent to my home office.

And wouldn't you know it, about two weeks later, after I got that notice, I realized I hadn't had a period. Right away, I took a urine test, and I was pregnant. I was also shocked, but I was definitely pregnant. The three different kinds of pregnancy tests I took confirmed it.

Before I told anyone, I made a doctor's appointment and said on the phone, "You will not believe this. I just took four pee tests, and it says I'm pregnant." My doctor said, "Come down this afternoon. We'll squeeze you in. Let's get blood work and see if this is true."

It shouldn't have been true. I was not on any meds. I was not on any progesterone. I was not on birth control because I thought *it's not going to happen. My left tube sucks. There's no way I'm getting pregnant.*

I headed to the doctor's office and sat on pins and needles for an hour or two, waiting for the results.

Sure enough, I was pregnant.

I drove home thinking, *what the hell?* And then I got happy, because I was like, *holy shit, God is going to give me a baby? I didn't even try, and God is going to give me a baby? You have got to be kidding me. Doing everything I need to do for everybody else is finally going to work? That's what I had to do? I had to put my ambitions, thought process, and whatever I wanted in life away and make everybody else around me happy? Shit, I would have done that ten years ago.*

I told Richard I was pregnant, and he told his grandparents.

The doctor, meanwhile, had told me she was going to do whatever she could to make sure I didn't have a miscarriage and lose this baby, but she told me that I also needed my husband's help. There was too much stress around me.

When I begged my husband to, "Please, do something to get your grandparents gone, because I've got to be on bed rest, and I can't have the stress of her constantly badgering me," he didn't rise to the occasion. I was a Realtor at the time, and his step-grandma called my broker so many times, telling my boss how bad of a piece of shit I was, that he called me and said if I could not get my personal life in order, I could no longer keep my real estate license with him.

I didn't understand what I was supposed to be a piece of a shit about.

I gave this woman an allowance every month. I did whatever she wanted me to do. I paid her electric bill because she was plugged into us. I tried to make sure we'd eat dinner every night as a family, so at least the grandparents had something to do.

The step-grandma would help with dinner by bringing over a side dish or dessert. She always had a smile on her face and never complained.

Richard and I thought his grandparents were happy. What she was pissed off about was that her house wasn't finished yet, but that wasn't our fault either. She also knew I had no control of the finances, so the person she should have been yelling at was my husband.

But at the same time, she did not want me to be happy. So she pressured me, and pressured me, and pressured me until one day, I broke and had a miscarriage.

To this day, I believe her constant badgering and making it where I could not get an ounce of sleep caused it.

I had nowhere to go.

Even when I went to see my mother, the step-grandma would follow me. She called my mother constantly and harassed her, too. I called the cops and tried to get a restraining order, but I had to be careful because we were illegally growing drugs at the time.

But instead of looking out for myself, I was looking out for everybody else while also trying to have this baby. I was trying not to be selfish when I should have been selfish during the time that I finally got pregnant.

What the hell was I thinking?

Now, I will never know whether if she left me alone, and I had just stayed on bedrest, and everything went smoothly if I would have had a miscarriage or not.

There's never going to be a time that I'm going to know that.

It could have happened either way.

It could have been the most perfect world for me, and everything would have been different, but maybe I still would have had the miscarriage.

In hindsight, I probably would have. I probably was not going to keep this baby either way. But that was still a part of my life that affected me greatly.

To recap, step-grandma was suing us for palimony; she was asking for one-third of our assets, even though she had only been married to Richard's grandfather for a short amount of time. Richard and I had created our lives years prior to having her enter them. What really shocked me was that my husband was really excited about the fifth baby. It was one of the few times that he showed excitement throughout the process. And one of the few times he'd shown excitement about anything that had to do with me.

In the public face of our marriage, we looked amazing. In the private part, we were not amazing. We fought every single day. Because even though he talked a lot of shit to me, and he would grab me, hit me, and hurt me, I still never kept my mouth shut. I still talked shit back to him.

But he did not help me get her to stop bugging me. A couple of times, he begged his grandfather to please help him stop his wife, but he didn't.

While she came at us, the grandfather was so devastated over the divorce proceedings that he stalked her! In retaliation, she thought if she came after us, we could make him stop. But we couldn't control his actions. We could ask him to stop, but we couldn't control him.

It was a vicious cycle, and one of us needed to say, "Stop, this needs to end." But we didn't. And so, probably, in the end, I would have lost that baby, regardless of the harassment happening. But the moment I had the miscarriage, I knew the grandmother caused another loss for me.

She would call me many times during the day and night just to tell me she would not rest until I lost my baby. When she succeeded, she was elated and at the news of my loss, called and laughed at me. She said I was never going to be a mother. That God would never let a worthless piece of shit, like me, ever have a child.

When I hung up, she immediately called back and laughed. I remember standing in my driveway, wishing I had the strength to kill myself.

Because she was right.

CHAPTER 7

He's My Left Arm

"I'd lost myself in the abyss of
someone else's tyranny."
–Cassandra Giovanni, Love Exactly

*L*ife after losing my fifth baby was surreal.

I went about my day like a robot.

I never had a smile on my face.

I went through the motions.

Getting up, making breakfast, feeding the animals.

I was defeated.

God had abandoned me.

Richard took out his frustrations on me by berating me or hitting me. The words "worthless" and "selfish" were all he ever said to me.

My situation was made more difficult by what was happening with my husband's step-grandma, who was suing us for palimony despite everything we had done for her and the grandpa.

It was difficult to grasp the fact that I would never be a mother. I no longer prayed every night and hadn't since I'd lost the first baby. I used to thank God for my life and my opportunities. I used to pray for silly things like rain, so I didn't have to go running because I hated running. Praying was a relief for me, but I just stopped believing in Him. I believed that He hated me. And the more I believed that, the more I self-destructed inside.

I was so angry at God that I told everyone, "God doesn't even exist." I still didn't say that I was an atheist because, in my heart, I knew God existed. But I would be like, "Gosh, whatever. God? Are you serious? Where's He at? He does not exist." AND I hated him. I mean, I *hated* God.

I hadn't prayed since the loss of my first child at twenty-seven. At thirty-four, I was done.

He'd made my life so damn miserable that not only was there no God. But I hated myself more, too, because I knew that that was a wrong way to think. Still, it was how I felt down to my bones.

Then I started doing drugs. I had smoked weed off and on, but now I was doing cocaine a lot. I don't know why I didn't just start drinking and why I did cocaine instead, but that's what happened. I ate anything I wanted and didn't exercise either. I'd lie in bed for hours on end.

My relationship with my parents bummed me out even more. I hated the fact that even though I knew my parents loved me, I simply wanted them to come to my house and have dinner with me. I wanted them to have Thanksgiving and Christmas with me and for them to be regular parents instead of me having to drive to see them because the drive was an hour and a half one way.

That didn't seem to matter because when I got to their house, my mother was miserable, talking only about how I'm "not good enough." How I was still living, "this lie of a relationship." My husband and I had been together since I was eighteen, and we were still doing the same thing. Nothing had progressed.

We were drug dealers with an illegal growing operation struggling financially. Where did the money go? It funded our stupid lifestyle and a lot of cocaine. After cocaine, I'd do any drug you put in front of me except for heroin or meth. I knew I was probably never going to come back from those kinds of drugs. So I guess the fact that I had at least a line that I wouldn't cross as a drug addict made me feel better than a drug addict. Maybe that's why I didn't think of myself that way—because of that line. But really, drug addicts have no line.

On top of drugs, I drank all the time.

The only saving grace was my animals that I adored and that I always made sure I took care of. I had three dogs that needed me. Coincidentally, my oldest dog, Mo Wrinkles, a Shar-Pei, who was usually an asshole and was eight or nine at the time, always had my back. He was around for every single baby that I lost, and each time that happened, he would curl up next to me and love on me. Dogs just know when their human parents are hurting. It meant a lot to me when he would lie with me because I knew that he could feel my sadness.

Mo Wrinkles was the one constant in my life. Then two years after I lost my last baby, and I was down one fallopian tube. I lost him to a kidney disease that Shar-Peis always get. We had been battling it for years, and I knew eventually, I would lose him, but when he died, it was like grieving my sixth baby.

A part of my life sealed up.

I'd known I couldn't have children for quite a while before he died and was trying to get over that, but Mo Wrinkles' death piled on top of everything else. That dog meant a lot to me. We made a casket for Mo Wrinkles, buried him in the backyard, and created a memorial. I sobbed.

During that time, everybody would always tell me, "Hey, go adopt. Go do this. Go do that." Or, they would say, "It wasn't meant to be." Once my mom told me that maybe everything had happened because "You're just not a good person to have a child," which was difficult to hear from her.

I continued the struggle of trying to move forward but was stuck. What made it so much harder was that whenever I would go someplace and somebody would have a kid, people had to ask me about my situation. Society said that I should have a child by my mid-thirties. Actually, I should have had 2.2 children in my life by then.

No matter where I went, I was asked, "How many kids do you have?" When I would reply, "None." The person would look at me and go, "Oh, that's too bad. You should get started. What are you waiting for?"

What was I supposed to say to that? Was I supposed to tell them my whole story? Originally, I would reply, "I would have loved to have kids, but I just lost five." Or, "We're not allowed to have kids." But my favorite line became "It's not for lack of trying."

I don't know how many times I thought about taking my life, and when I didn't, I would be down on myself because I didn't even have the courage to end my misery.

With the step-grandma suing us for palimony, we were running out of money, trying to fight her. And we were still trying to finish the grandparents' house because the logic was, *if we finish this house, everything will be fine. They can be out of the RV. She'll be happy. She'll get what she wants.* I hoped we'd all be back to what we considered "normal." But I knew my life was nowhere near that.

We had to sell our horses. And when we did, I thought of my lost children. Every time I'd lost a child, my animals had been there for me. And thank goodness I had Mo Wrinkles in my life because if I hadn't, I might have gone through with killing myself years prior. But the more dogs I had, the more I thought, *who's going to take care of them?* I felt it must be similar to what parents think if they die before their children: *who's going to take care of them?*

You would think that my friends and all the people who knew the truth about us would make a tight-knit community, but that wasn't the case. We were tightknit in a sense because we all trusted each other to a certain point, but we each had limits. I thought my job was always to keep everybody happy. So I did whatever that meant.

Then my husband said, "Let's go to a group sex party." To which I said, "What?" "Let's go to a group sex club," he said. "Let's be swingers." I asked, "Where's this coming from?" So shocked that he would say that—shocked because sex had never been an issue between us throughout the years. We'd always had it. It was everything else in our life that was the issue.

I couldn't help thinking: *because that's the cure-all. Having sex with random people at a party is an absolute way to fix your marriage. Not therapy, right? We're too good for therapy. Not delving into what's really going on in our marriage, you, being an abuser, me, an enabler who allows the abuse to keep happening.*

I was too scared to leave him because what was I going to do? I didn't know anything else. Being with him and running our business was my whole adult life.

I thought *I have to do this because I need his direction. I need him in my life. He's my left arm.*

But one day, it felt like something was off with him. Because the one thing I thought I had with him was trust. Now, I'm not a jealous person, so if he talked to a girl, I didn't care. I trusted him with my life because he was running it. Never once did I think he would step outside our marriage until he started acting a little weird. I couldn't put my finger on what was causing his new behavior, so I checked our cell phone records and saw a phone number I didn't recognize. When I called it, a girl answered.

That was unusual because he was very adamant about never talking to anybody outside of our circle—and they were all guys.

When I called Richard to ask him about it, his phone was off. I tried again, and his phone was off again. It was unusual. I kept trying his number throughout the day. Then when I called her number, it was off, too.

He didn't come home that night. And he'd never not come home before. When I called our "friends," they were vague. "Oh, we haven't seen him. We don't know." I knew something out of the ordinary was going on. These people had come to my house every single day for I don't know how many years—but in the last couple of days, I hadn't seen anybody. I hadn't talked to anybody. When I heard that girl's voice on her message, my world shattered. I knew right then and there; Richard had cheated on me. It was the absolute most heartbreaking thing I have ever felt.

After eighteen years of marriage, my husband cheated on me. After eighteen years of hearing him tell me I was worthless, eighteen years of him throwing a punch against me here and there, and the bruises and the pain. Eighteen years of keeping my dreams at bay so he could live his, and being so unhappy, and he'd cheated on me.

I'd let his step-grandma stress me out to the point where I'd lost my one chance of having a child, and he'd cheated on me with some girl.

It didn't even matter who she was or where he'd met her.

What mattered was how I reacted. I acted like it was the worst thing that could have happened to me. And then I stopped and realized that I was more devastated about him cheating than I was about losing my first child. That realization drove home the point that I was a piece of shit and wasn't worthy of anything.

After all I have done for you, you just walked out of our marriage? You didn't even have the balls to tell me you were done? This is my thanks?

Instead of telling myself, *this isn't your fault, Toni, this is not your fault*, I badgered myself, *what did I do wrong?*

When I remember that moment, I ask myself, *what the fuck was I thinking?* That should have been the moment that I took all of his stuff and put it out front in a big old pile and lit that shit on fire. Our "friends" thought that's what I would do because I'd always talked this big game. "Oh, if he ever cheated on me, he'd be gone." "If he ever raised his hand to me and hit me, I'd punch him." "If he ever called me a name, I'd tell him to go fuck himself." But I didn't do any of that.

I didn't get angry. Instead, I sat in the living room day in and day out and cried.

I wasn't scared to talk shit to a stranger if they came and talked shit to me. But Richard was doing the exact same stuff I said I would kick his ass for, and I did nothing. He would call me names at night, and I would sit there and look at the floor while he'd yell, "Look at me while I'm talking to you." Then I'd look at him with my lip quivering, trying not to cry, and he would yell at me again, "Stop fucking crying. This is your fault."

The moment I had that door open, I should have grabbed his stuff and torched it. I should have taken my stuff and my three dogs, loaded up my car, and left. I should have taken all the cash that was in the house and filed for divorce the next day. That's what I should have done. That's what a lot of women would have said I should have done. It's what a lot of women also don't do.

I bawled like I had never cried before when I found out that he was cheating on me.

When he finally came home after two days, I said, "I can't believe you're cheating on me. Who is she?" But he wouldn't tell me. Instead, he moved out of our shared bedroom into the guest room.

And here's what's funny.

As if it cannot get any lower than him cheating on me, when he moved out to the guest room, before he left to go to work that day, he asked me to transfer his clothes from our bedroom closet into the guest room closet. *Can I set his room up?* And do you know what I spent the day doing? Moving his stuff into that room and organizing it for him. That's what I did. I cried the entire time doing it. But I did it.

While Richard was out in the guest room, I was still trying to be intimate with him because I thought *maybe I'm not giving it to him enough.* Although we had sex all the time, when all of a sudden, we weren't having sex, I thought he needed more.

One night, he gave in to me, and we were intimate. In mid-action, I said, "Are you not enjoying this?" He replied, "I feel like I'm cheating on my girlfriend." I was married to a man who told me in mid-sexual action that he was "cheating on his girlfriend." Richard finished, and I got up feeling lower than a whore. He dressed and went to his girlfriend's house.

His new pattern was coming home after work, showering, and going to his girlfriend's house. He spent weekends with her and took her on motorcycle rides with our friends. He went on weekend trips that we would have gone on with our friends, flaunting her like she was his next new wife.

I looked at my friends who were supposed to be there for me.

They were the "circle of trust friends" and made up a network that you're not supposed to go out of. They were all on his side. None of them supported me. Not one.

They were all scared that if they didn't support him, we would all get busted for what we did for a living. Our "work."

None of them would tell me anything, despite the fact that I had been a part of their lives every day for the past fifteen years. I had been there for their breakups and their sob stories. I had hugged them and given them advice. I had been there in every way you could possibly imagine as a friend. Now, I couldn't get them to walk into my house and say hi to me.

Not only had I lost my husband, I'd lost the circle and was all alone. My "friends" only wanted to make sure I didn't wig out and ruin the businesses.

About a month later, Richard and I got into a big argument. Every time he'd come home, we would fight. It was physical. There were times I thought he was going to break my arm. He would hit me and pull my hair, and it was probably the most physical we had been in such a short amount of time. It would get heated quick between us because I could not get him to realize he was making a mistake by being with that girl.

I berated myself; *why can't I just leave him alone? He doesn't want me anymore, and I'm being treated like dirt.* I did everything I could to throw myself at him and asked him, "What does she have that I don't?" That's when he looked at me and said, "She has a kid." Then he drove the knife in deeper when he asked me, "We don't have children. We don't have a family, so what are you and I doing?"

She has a kid. Man, I was so heartbroken when he said that to me.

Then my so-called friends repeated to me what he said! "She can give him what you can't."

That's when I stopped eating.

I would go days without eating and then do hot yoga for ninety minutes, hoping that it would give my mind release. When I got home, I would drink some water, and that would be it! I lost twenty-five pounds in a month.

One day, after coming home from a date with the girl, Richard looked me up and down and said, "Wow, you are so skinny, and you have makeup on. Aren't you beautiful?" Hearing his words gave me hope. *This is going to make my life better again. I'm going to feel love again.* Those were the thoughts that leapt to my mind. Now, I look back at that person and think *God, why did I let myself get disrespected so badly?*

That was the angriest I'd ever been at God. But I was still trying desperately to hold onto something. I still got up and walked five miles with my dogs on the property and then walked them home. I still took care of them. Before Mo Wrinkles passed, he knew what my husband had done, or maybe he sensed that Richard was a bad guy.

Mo Wrinkles sat next to me all time and was an asshole to Richard. The other dogs, Rocky and Titus, followed suit. They didn't want any part of Richard. He was never home anyway. But I was still there. I was still doing his laundry. I was still fixing his bed and making him dinner like a fucking idiot—hoping he'd come home.

Shortly after that bad fight, that's when Richard suggested we do some swinging.

It was New Year's Eve. We went to a party in San Francisco with another couple. The entire time we were there, all he wanted to do was find another girl so we could be swingers that night. And all I wanted was whatever it took to make him happy because having him happy would make my life better again.

That night someone took a picture of me. I was standing in a dress, trying to look happy. I'm smiling, but I can still remember how horrible I felt about myself. The next day as we drove back, Richard yelled at me all the way home because I couldn't find anybody to join us.

Richard and I weren't apart for longer than twelve hours in eighteen years up until he cheated on me. So, after all the cheating and lies, when he said, "I'm going to break it off with her, but we're going to be swingers," I said, "Okay, where do we go? How do we this? Show me where we can become swingers. Is there a website? Let's make this happen."

I was jealous that he was with that girl, but when we started doing the swinger thing, I enjoyed it. And it wasn't necessarily because it was helping our marriage.

I enjoyed it because it was dangerous.

At the good swinger clubs, people are checked. They wear condoms, and it's very respectful. If you don't want to touch a person, they move on. You don't have a group gang bang. There are a lot of rules you have to abide by, and there are people on hand to make sure the rules are followed. If you can't abide by the rules, they kick you out. This was a very respectful way to be swingers. People who choose this and have it as their lifestyle in their relationship, that's awesome.

All of a sudden, I was loving it. Not because of the sex, but I loved getting the attention from men and women. Now, I know I'm bisexual. My husband knew I was always bisexual. But I was getting attention from people telling me I was beautiful. They accepted me for me. The world opened up.

I talked to women outside the group of guys I had been with all those years. I listened to their lives and connected with them. I shared an emotional bond with them and actually liked it.

Before I knew it, I was having sex with multiple men and not even caring whether or not they were using protection. On a trip to Vegas, I got a stupid fucking tramp stamp that said "swinger." All I was doing was destroying myself.

I've since had it covered up and have a really beautiful piece on my body. That period of my life represents one bad decision after another. At the same time, people were *still* asking me about babies. People were *still* trying to get me to adopt. My mom was *still* trying to get me to use the Indian surrogate.

I knew God didn't like what I was up to. I was still doing a whole lot of cocaine. I did so much that I could even sleep after doing it. But then I did so much that it didn't give me the same effect as before. I became a functional cocaine addict. I could sleep. I could eat. I could do whatever I wanted. I just needed that little bump to get me going. I reasoned *I can do all the things I did before, so what's a little bump? I'm not a drug addict. I'm still above a drug addict.*

One night we went to a few swinger parties with couples we were steady with. That went on for about three months. But that night, I reconnected with a girl named Beatrice, who I'd known when we were kids. I'd had a crush on her then.

We'd reconnected once before when Facebook came around. I knew she'd had a crush on me in high school, too.

At that time, I was in my twenties. She actually brought me to my first concert, Def Leppard. And while I knew then that she had a crush on me, I was with my husband at the time. We respected that boundary.

Then I met her again while we were swingers, and Beatrice and I went out to dinner and dancing.

It was confusing because I was being a swinger with my husband and trying to make things work, and she knew that.

Then one night, my husband and I went to the strip club. In between all the swinger stuff, we started to talk about the loss of our babies. I found out that he was mourning. He told me how every time I'd come home and told him I'd lost a baby, he'd cried. He said he'd wanted to go with me to every one of those appointments, but he didn't feel like he could be strong enough.

Now, I don't know if he told me this because he thought it was what I wanted to hear, and he was trying to keep ahold of me. But it *was* what I wanted to hear. I felt closer to him again. The more I felt that way it seemed, the more he told me. I was doing what he wanted. I was back that night.

Until I wasn't.

When we drove home from the strip club, I snapped for some reason and let him have it in the car. I told him off about every little thing he'd ever made me feel. I told him how much I hated him.

My words poured out so fast and loud. It felt so good to get it all out and tell him what a bastard he was. How small he was because of all the bad things he would say to me. That he pushed me down even though I was smarter than him. How he never wanted me to succeed in life, and the only way to keep me down was to beat me down. How bad he was as a person to let me go through the loss of five of those babies all alone. How he let his grandparents beat me down so badly that I lost our fifth child.

I screamed at him as he drove, getting it all out, releasing, finally, years of agony. How when he hit our dog, I had to take him to a vet that was two hours away every single day for six months for treatment. How he wasn't even there for the dog. It just kept coming out.

Then he turned toward me, stared me down in the car, and punched me so damn hard on my left side that my head hit the door. He held my head down and just kept punching me and punching me and yelling, "Is this what you want? Is this what you want? Is this the attention you want?" He did that for thirty minutes all the way home.

I cowered with my hand over my head, screaming at him to stop and that I was sorry. "I didn't mean any of it! Stop! Please stop! You're hurting me! This is the worst you've ever done it. Stop. You're hurting me. You're hurting me. You're making my ears bleed. Please stop. I have to see my mom tomorrow in the hospital. You're going to give me a black eye..."

But he just kept grabbing my hair and banging my head against the car door, telling me he didn't care. Punching my side. Grabbing the seatbelt and choking me with it. That's when I made the decision that as soon as I could, I was leaving him.

That was the last damn time he was going to touch me and make me feel like I was a piece of shit because I couldn't give him what he wanted—a family. And I couldn't give me what I wanted—kids. I was no longer going to sit there and have him do this to me.

It was over.

"We need silence to be able to touch souls."
– Mother Teresa

When I left Richard, I went to the apartment of my old friend from high school, Beatrice, who I'd had a crush on and who'd had a crush on me—the one I'd been to dinner and dancing with.

She had hopes that she and I could finally explore the feelings we had both harbored for so long.

That worked.

But she had also re-entered my life when I really needed someone.

That worked, too.

I woke up the next day with the left side of my face bruised, beaten, and swollen. I couldn't see out of my left eye. My ear was bleeding. But I had to go see my mom and dad because my mom had just had knee replacement surgery, so I had to visit.

After I put makeup on, I saw my mom in the hospital. Even

with makeup, you could tell my face was bruised because my left eye was swollen, and I was still black and blue. My cheek was swollen. I had a cut on my lip. On my entire left side, I was totally torn up. In some spots on my head, you could see where my husband had pulled out my hair.

I told my mom a story that I had been riding my dirt bike on my property, didn't have my helmet on when I hit a bump, and my face smashed into the handlebars.

I don't know to this day if she believed me or not, but she didn't question me. I don't know if she would have known if she would have said anything either. Instead, she said, "It looks like that hurts a lot. Hope you won't do that again." I said, "No, I'll never ride a motorcycle without a helmet again."

Her response was an analogy to me. She didn't go any further because she knew I was hurting. Since I'm not a mother, I don't know if she had a sense of what was wrong. But I would venture to say because I am her only child that she probably knew, and she probably also knew not to push it any further and instead to give me that analogy. We've never talked about that moment again. I never told her this part of the story.

Also that weekend, my husband went back to that girl, and they took off on a weekend trip to a car show in Reno.

One of my friends who didn't agree with Richard's treatment and the way he was parading his new girlfriend around came over to check on me one day. When he saw my face, he was so angry at what had happened and asked, "Why are you letting this happen?" I had no answer. When I had no answer, he just hugged me in the biggest, longest hug and let me cry. He didn't even say anything the whole time he was hugging me. As he let me go, he said, "You deserve so much better." Then he left.

If I hadn't had those three dogs, I would have hung myself. I would have overdosed. I would've done whatever it took to kill myself. Those dogs saved my life. And when that friend of ours came over and gave me that hug, that meant the world to me.

After that weekend and the last time my husband put his hands on me, although it was sudden, I moved in with the woman who would become my girlfriend. The joke is, when you sleep with a lesbian, you better get your U-Haul because you're moving in, and that's what happened. I was in that relationship with her for six years. I loved her, and she loved me. There was never any abuse. She was just an alcoholic, which I knew. But then I became an alcoholic, who was still doing lots of cocaine.

As I added alcohol to the mix, I ate tons of crap on top of it. I was no longer jogging. I was longer fit. I didn't care about what happened to me. I was just getting up and starting my day with a screwdriver, a line of cocaine, and McDonald's. I was broke and mooching off this girl. I felt so bad, but that didn't stop me.

Shortly after I moved in and before the shit really hit the fan, I told my parents I was bisexual.

I couldn't even face them to tell them. I actually told them over the phone, saying, "Hey, you remember that girl in high school? I was in band class with her?" They said, "Yeah," and I explained a little bit about her so they could jog their memories because it had been so many years. Then I announced, "Well, we're dating." My parents' reaction was: "What? You're what?" I said, "I've known for most of my life that I'm bisexual, and we're dating now." My parents were speechless; they didn't say much. My dad was more accepting of it, and he said, "Okay," as the more loving one between the two of them. My mom couldn't utter a word.

After what felt like five minutes of silence, which was probably five seconds, my mom said, "But you were always against gay marriage." I said, "The ones who are usually the most against it tend to be the ones who are in the closet. Love is love, Mom. I love her, and she loves me. I'm attracted to her, and I want to be with her." My mom replied, "Well, I can never accept it, but if it makes you happy, then it makes you happy."

My girlfriend took a different approach with my mom. Whatever my mother's view was, she was accepting of it. This was nice because, for once, I felt like things were looking up for me. Yes, I still had issues to deal with. I was still doing cocaine, not as much as I had been, but I was still doing it.

Life plodded along.

As a drug addict, I was great at hiding it.

Of course, as soon as my husband realized I was as happy as I possibly could be, he wanted to seek therapy with me. He contacted me all the time, wanting to see me. He also fueled my drug habit because I was getting my cocaine through him. Doing that was a way for him to still control me. It was a way for him to continue to see me so he could convince me that he was better than the girl I was with. When he called and said, "Let's do this." I said, "No, I'm with someone who's healthy. She's showing me what love is. I don't want to be with you."

This went on for a few months until he started dating a girl way younger than him. By this time, he was almost in his forties, and that girl was twenty-three. He thought his doing that was going to affect me. But that backfired because I thought, *oh good, he's dating somebody else. He's moving on.*

His attempts to try and make me jealous so I would come home didn't work. As I've said, I'm not a jealous person. I wasn't really jealous of the first girlfriend in retrospect. I was jealous that he could have a relationship with another woman when he was supposed to be married to me. I was jealous that she had a child and could give him what I couldn't.

But soon, everything around me closed in. Life got harder and harder. It wasn't *finally going my way* after all.

My husband stopped giving me money. He was supposed to give me alimony, but he cut me off. He would give me cocaine but would cut me off on money. So I struggled to figure out how to pay bills.

Richard did give me a car to drive, and I was grateful, thinking, *wow, he does care about me.* Little did I know, the car had been originally bought for his girlfriend. And guess how I found out...the repo man.

Yes, you read that right...the repo man.

One early morning, around 1 am, I heard a bang on the front door. When I opened the door, and the poor guy saw my face, he asked me who I was. I could tell by the confused look in his eyes that he was expecting to see someone else. When I explained who I was, he took a deep breath and said, "I hate to do this to you, but I feel like I should tell you this. I have to repo this car. The gentleman who bought this car had a different lady with him. From the shocked look on your face seeing me, you had no idea he had bought this car for his girlfriend. I am so very sorry to give you this news." As he finished his sentence, he looked down at his muddy boots. Then after, what seemed like five minutes, he broke through the awkward silence and said, "Let's go get your stuff out of the car."

The virtual slap in the face was powerful, and it hurt. This big, burly man was taking the one possession I thought I had, and with his solemn voice, was trying to make me feel whole.

Richard's mistreatment was so blatant. I was getting slapped in the face more and more.

I was pissed to lose that car because I had solely lived off what we did for work with the farm. And yes, I had a real estate license and did very well when he allowed me to work in that capacity, but without the car, I couldn't even work.

I felt there could be no rockier bottom for me. Without a

vehicle, I had to walk everywhere and try even harder to figure things out.

Nothing was working.

One day I knew I had to move. That I could not be in the same state as Richard anymore.

For what I was planning, I felt like certain people in the new state where I was going could help.

But I had never moved across the country. Still, I had to go.

I told Beatrice, "Look, I'm moving to Florida. I've got to start my life over again. I can't be in California anymore. I've got to go. I think I have this opportunity there." She wanted to come with, I told her she shouldn't, but she did anyway. She had my back and told me she loved me. I guessed this was what love was. I had to figure out a way to get the money we'd need to move and settled on having a big garage sale,

In Sarasota, Florida, I had family. It was my husband's family, but he never talked to them. I was the one who was mostly close to his side of the family. I actually considered his cousin a close friend of mine. I moved to Florida, thinking I would have a little bit of help from them, but in the end, they sided with him because blood was thicker than water. I lost someone who I thought was my brother—that cousin—who didn't feel the same way as I did.

Even though my husband couldn't have cared less about what happened to his family, and the only reason why he had any relationship with them was because of me, it was another blow. All our "friends" were no longer in my life, either.

If anything, they wanted me to stay with my husband because they were scared of what he might do to their businesses. They were trying to make that my problem and make me feel guilty. I did feel guilty for not doing what I felt like I should be doing, but at the same time, I needed to look after myself.

Once in Florida, I filed for divorce. Then even though we had amicably agreed I was to get all my personal belongings out of the house and could have half our assets in lieu of alimony, he sold all my stuff.

Forget keeping that deal that he made with me about giving me half the assets and all of my possessions. He sold everything... the jewelry that my mom had given me that had been in her family, my baby piano that I had loved so much, memories of when we opened our first business, every piece of heavy equipment we owed, all my possessions that held my memories, gone. It was all gone, and I had no money, no business, nothing. Because he had sold it all for pennies on the dollar. Of course, whatever he couldn't sell, he burned.

He said he had supported me for eighteen years, and it was now time for me to support myself. I remarked back, "Like I need to get a higher pain threshold?" Yes, I still brought that up.

I stated, "So, after all the years where I supported you in every way possible that you could possibly think of, and me losing five babies virtually on my own, this is what you do." The words came out fast again "I stuck by you for all of these years, helped you in every way possible to make your business work, and was loyal to you. I never deviated from you. I had your back. I was emotionally there for you when you were never emotionally there for me. I was physically there for you when you were never physically there for me. When you were down, I was down deeper. When you were up, I was holding you up. I put your world and you on a pedestal, and you're going to tell me after eighteen years you supported me? NOW it's time for me to go? What do you want me to do? How am I supposed to get by?"

Richard didn't want to sign the divorce papers because he was pissed that I was going to keep my maiden name. He wanted me to keep my married name, which tells me he still wanted to control some aspect of my life.

So I hustled because I was always a hustler.

And I've always known I'm smart.

I had a brain; it was just for some damn reason I hadn't used it for nearly twenty years.

I figured out a way to get some money so I could live. Richard gave me a little money here and there, but I needed more to survive.

Then he finally agreed to sign the divorce papers.

It was two years after I'd filed for divorce.

He only signed because he'd met someone his age. She also had a kid. Finance-wise, she was doing fine. He wanted to get married to her ASAP. That's why he signed the divorce papers.

He was supposed to give me alimony.

He didn't.

My car got repoed.

All the houses and properties we owned were in foreclosure.

I also found out he hadn't paid our back taxes for many years and that we owed thousands and thousands of dollars in back taxes.

Then there was another little development. As our divorce was finalizing, he moved to Florida, too!

I wanted to be away from him so badly, and when he moved across the country to Florida, I got scared. He still tried to get me to go to therapy. He still told me I needed to be with him, not my girlfriend. And as all of this was going on, I was struggling to pay the rent because the money I thought I was going to get from him wasn't coming.

So, even though I had my Florida real estate license, I took a job at TJ Maxx.

I was an almost-40-year-old woman starting over at TJ Maxx.

But it wasn't as simple as pulling myself up by my bootstraps. Life was about to get way harder before it got easier.

Sure, I made just enough to barely pay rent (sometimes), but I had no car because it had been repoed. So I had to take the bus. It took me two hours to get to work and two to get home. At times, I had to beg the landlord to let me miss rent because I needed it for food.

When I reached out to my mother and father, they wouldn't help me financially. My mother said, "You put yourself in this position, so you need to figure it out."

But I was trying to do that, and it wasn't working.

I'd gotten my real estate license in Florida because that was the one thing I knew how to do. I knew about real estate. I knew about construction. But it takes money to get going in real estate, so I had to work at TJ Maxx.

Working in retail is a son of a bitch. You're on your feet all time. I was still overweight by probably 200 pounds and still eating like shit, trying to make it on my poor little feet standing up all day.

The customers were tough, and it wasn't rewarding because people complain.

My life was work all the time. Take the bus home. Pick up the phonebook to cold call expired listings. I did whatever I needed to do to get listings and kick things in the ass in the real estate world. I was trying as hard as possible to make ends meet.

I got on food stamps to eat. I was trying to pay rent, and my girlfriend was working, too. Her job in California had told her that she could work remotely from Florida, but she wound up not being able to do that. Then she was struggling to find a job also.

I felt bad because the weight of her deciding to follow me was affecting her career and life.

This made me more devastated.

My thoughts were toxic again: *I can't get my shit straight, and now I'm messing up somebody else's shit.*

But weirdly, it was almost comforting to have someone else go through the same scenario with me, which was horrible to even think about. But I can't deny it was a comfort.

In the meantime, my ex had remarried, although he had only known his new wife a couple of months.

I also had a brokerage that was very supportive, and I don't know if Steve, who owned it, knows to this day how supportive he was. I never told anyone what I was going through, but he knew something was up. He knew I was struggling. I've never divulged the truth about that part of my history until right now in writing this book.

No one knew I was on food stamps when I was in Florida. I was so embarrassed to ask for help. And I was one day away from being homeless. During that time, I know God was there helping me, but I still hated Him. I still blamed Him for my situation.

Now, I can see the truth.

God was helping me because I never physically laid underneath an overpass or on the street. Yes, I had to ask for help and be on food stamps. But He also put me in touch with Steve.

I thank God for Steve and that I'd placed my real estate license with him.

CHAPTER 9

Taking Chances

Life is too short to wake up in the morning
with regrets... If you get a chance, take it.
If it changes your life, let it.
— Unknown

When I had a chance to interview with one of the new home builders in Florida, I made the decision that I needed to also leave Florida. It was time to take advantage of opportunities in Texas.

Moving also meant my girlfriend could move to Austin, Texas, with me. The bigger picture was that I wanted to make my life a little better. So I made the leap and told the company in Florida that I was going to be moving to Austin shortly. They said, "We could set you up with an interview. You can even finish the interview process in Austin and then secure a position."

It was the first time it seemed something could go my way

and stick. I could not believe my luck as I said, "Yes, absolutely. Set me up with that interview. I'll be down there in about two weeks." They said, "No problem." And then, "We're going to need a couple of professional references." To that, I thought, *fuck, I don't have any.*

The only person I knew in a professional capacity was my broker, Steve, and he was about to go on vacation to Canada. I had to act fast.

When I asked him if there was any way that he could help me out and give me a recommendation, he didn't hesitate and said, "Absolutely. No problem. You have been an asset to this company."

I've been an asset to this company? I've probably made two or three sales.

I hadn't been there very long, so I didn't think I'd done much. I felt like he had probably spent more money on me having my license with his brokerage than I was making him.

He urged me: "But I've got to do it soon. I'm leaving."

Well, he went on vacation, and the people who needed to talk to him couldn't get ahold of him because they'd called him too late, and he was in Canada. So I emailed him and said, "They've been trying to call you," and he replied, "Oh, okay. You know what? Give me a second, and I'll call them back."

This guy hustled and worked long hours. Once a year, he went on a big vacation with his family, but there he was taking ten minutes out of his family time to call a company up and give them a reference for me. I don't remember if I did thank him. Everything was such a whirlwind. I was in shock that anyone would even try to help me. I was in shock that God was showing me a path. I couldn't get over hoping *this is actually going to make a difference.*

I'm grateful for Steve. He did help me on this path to get to where I'm at today, and he doesn't know that. I should have told him.

With the recommendation delivered, my girlfriend and I packed up the U-Haul, loaded up our three dogs, and drove out to Austin. When we got there, we had no idea what Austin looked like. We had no idea where to move.

Without a clue about any of the neighborhoods, we hired an apartment locator from Craigslist. We told them where my job was going to be and that we needed the cheapest apartment you could get. So the guy found us one. Sure, we had barely enough money and were still on food stamps, and cutting coupons to get food from Burger King, and every other little thing, but we were there. We knew if everything was going to work out, we had to go to work. That was the plan.

On my first day, I went to my interview, and wouldn't you know it before I walked into it, I had a couple of drinks. Even though I wasn't doing drugs anymore and had been cut off since I moved to Florida when I was no longer speaking to my ex-husband, I was still drinking.

No matter how many times my ex tried to get ahold of me when I lived in Florida and made excuses to reach me, such as, "How is Rocky doing? How is Titus doing?" I didn't bite. As if all of a sudden, it was his responsibility to know what was going on. I knew it was just a way to try to connect with me. To keep a grip on me. I rejected his efforts.

So I had no more ties with him, but yeah, I was drinking.

But wait...it gets better.

I drank more to make up for my lost drug habit. I'd become an alcoholic to the point where I could function.

So I'd had a couple of beers at a local bar right across the street before my interview, and then I went in nervous. It was my first interview for a corporation.

Yes, I'd had the TJ Maxx interview, but that was a fairly easy one.

This was a three-panel interview with questions coming at me in all sorts of ways. I had to have the right answers because I needed this job—especially because I had spent nearly the last two decades of my life growing drugs.

That had been my main occupation. Construction was our side business, and I had a real estate license. But for the most part, my public persona was not the same as my personal persona. I had to get through the interview and get the job.

That's what happened!

What a relief!

All I had to do then was make sales and keep my head down. I was going to be okay because I knew how to hustle and sell. So I knew I could do the job.

What I didn't know is if I could handle my alcohol.

I was drinking all the time.

Drinking in the morning.

Drinking at lunch.

Drinking when I got home.

Going out with newfound friends drinking.

The excuse I fell back on was *this is sales. It's what we do. We have a very stressful career. We have numbers to make. We have people to please. Customers who are always yelling at us. We need to drink.*

Finally, after some time had passed, I got off food stamps but was still eating like shit. Burger King, Pizza Hut, Subway, I was eating all the fast food. And I was up to a hundred pounds over-weight by then. I was really struggling, and so I started praying every night again.

I was ready to pray again regularly because God had shown me a light. Yet I was still destroying myself.

I was still fixated on the past and the question, *why did I let this happen to me?*

When I went back in time, a memory would pop up of people asking me why I didn't have children. Sometimes it wasn't my memory but life that messed with me. I would see someone with a baby, or a person would ask me why I didn't have children. This was natural, I know because I was in a new town meeting new people, so of course, they all asked me, "Why don't you have kids?"

I was back to that reality again.

It was brutal.

It robbed me of my self-esteem once more. I questioned my worth.

The move was not an escape from those questions and the memories that haunted me.

Instead of my go-to line of "It's not for a lack of trying," my new retort was, "We just didn't have any." But I still didn't confront my past. No, I was drinking it away.

Something had to change.

I just didn't know where to start.

I didn't know what to do, and I didn't want to admit what was going on with me. That I'd stayed in an abusive marriage. That I'd I lost five children.

I was ashamed of that part of my life, but it was such a big chunk of my existence. I was trying to hide the majority of my life, but I would never heal that way.

Besides that, I had a real shot at finally getting my finances together. I could make really great money, but if I didn't stop drinking, I was going to ruin it. I also had found a way to start using cocaine again. Drug addicts always find a way to become addicts again. My thoughts were fleeting, passing through my head while I ran around doing drugs again and drinking.

One drug-fueled night I was partying with some guy. I didn't even know who he was, but I met him at the bar. Somehow or another, we ended up in a part of Austin that I can't remember. It's a blur, but it was someplace downtown. We got into a car wreck.

I don't know how we didn't get arrested. I don't know how I got back to the bar to drive myself home. But we could have killed someone, and that would have been a blur, too.

I was destroying myself, depressed, and blaming myself for everything in my life. I knew I had to get better, and for that to happen, I had to love myself. I had to love the world. But even after that experience, my life was on replay.

As soon as I walked in the door, I couldn't drink fast enough. I drank until I passed out, and then I'd wake up and do it again.

During this time, I also noticed that my periods were getting heavier and heavier. I was changing a tampon or pad every hour. This new bodily habit of mine couldn't continue to exist. So I went to a new doctor and gave her my history.

I briefly explained the five pregnancies, and she said, "We're going to do a procedure called an ablation. If you're absolutely positive you're not going to have children, and you don't want to try doing it with a fertilized egg from a Petri dish, then we need to do this ablation. It will help your periods immensely."

When you have an ablation, they put you under and sear your uterus, like a piece of steak. When I found that out, I didn't hesitate and said, "No problem. That sounds like what I need to do. If it's going to stop the periods, we're going to do that!"

I had the ablation around October of 2016. The procedure was fine, and so was the recovery. You need very little time and can get up the next day. You don't even have an overnight stay. You can have the ablation in the morning and leave at night. When you get home, you'll have some cramping for a few days, but you can go back to life as usual for the most part. I was advised to "take it easy for a couple of weeks."

When November came along, I had a lot of pain around the time I was supposed to have my period. I was doubled over, and it felt just as bad as having my first ectopic pregnancy. I told my partner, "You need to take me to the emergency room."

Talking about my pain was different with her because I never had to hide it. Even though we were both drinking a lot, and she had her own emotional issues to deal with, she showed me what love was. Every time I had a problem and needed a partner, she was there. She demonstrated to me what loving was and how good it felt.

So when I felt that pain, I didn't hesitate to tell her. I knew she wasn't going to judge me. I knew she wasn't going to say, "Well, drive yourself to the hospital," even though we were only five minutes away. No, no. She got in the car. She said, "Get in. We're going."

When we got there, they had me lie down. I told the doctor what procedure I'd just had, and the emergency room staff person said, "Oh, you're not supposed to have pain. Your body is still trying to have a period. It's not supposed to be that way."

They immediately gave me a morphine drip, and since it was daytime, they called my doctor, who was in her office. She walked over and told me, "If you're having pain, it's not usual, not after having an ablation. Let's get you through these next couple of days. I'm going to give you some pain pills but just stay here until the pain subsides. Then make an appointment for next week. I want you to schedule it now because we need to discuss you having a hysterectomy. This pain is not going to stop."

She paused for a minute, met my eyes, and then said, "Honestly, if you're having this pain after ablation added to the hassle you had with losing your babies, it's probably because you have a rare disease. It's the opposite of endometriosis, but the only way to find out if you have it is by having a hysterectomy. There's no other way to look in your body and see if you have this disease other than when you have the hysterectomy, and they do a pathology test."

The next thing she said, I will never forget: "I have a feeling that's what you have and that none of the ectopic pregnancies and miscarriages were ever your fault, but let's discuss this further."

That was the first time I'd heard that all of the losses and all of the pain were not my fault. I knew then what I had gone through wasn't due to God punishing me for living a life of sin. He wasn't punishing me for being loyal to Richard. Could it be that *I was just meant to have all this tragedy and hardship for a reason?*

I'd only met that female doctor a year ago, so she didn't really know me. She knew about the babies because she'd needed my health history, but she didn't know everything else I'd experienced.

Yet, she stood there, telling me that everything I had been through was not my fault.

Again I thought, *there's no way. She has no idea.* Then I thought, *was this not God's fault then? Is this really and truly not my fault?*

After going back and forth with her a little bit more, I made an appointment with her and went home. Once home, I went on every forum you could possibly think of to learn whether or not having a hysterectomy was the right move for me.

Should I do it?

It was and is a big operation. I was losing an organ.

After weighing everything, I made the appointment to have the surgery in December of 2016.

CHAPTER 10

Look at Me Now

*"Look at me! Look at me! Look at me
NOW! It is fun to have fun, but
you have to know how."*
–The Cat in the Hat, Dr. Seuss

In December, while I was gearing up for my operation and figuring out my personal life, my professional life was going great.

I'd since moved on from the first company I had worked for and started with another company.

I had done so well with my first company that a second home builder recruited me. I was slowly chipping away at my debt, too.

Still, I had to file for bankruptcy in 2014, when I first moved to Austin. But when I filed, I found all sorts of items that I didn't realize I owed because the true financial disaster that was my life came out during the bankruptcy proceedings when I was getting all the paperwork ready.

I didn't realize that my ex-husband had really done a number on my credit. He did a number on everything. We had tax liens on a houseboat. We had tax liens on a boat. We had tax liens on cars. There were thousands and thousands and thousands of dollars in tax liens and back taxes, more than I had realized when I had initially filed for divorce. He had racked up millions.

A couple of years later, after the filing, I was doing pretty well. I had started over, financially, and saved up enough money to purchase my own home. This was very liberating for me because it was the first time I could purchase something on my own. It was the very first thing that I ever did for myself with my hard work, brains, and ability to take care of myself. It was also a "Ha-ha, asshole. You always said I couldn't do anything for myself. That I needed you to make sure I could do it, and without you, I would be nothing. Look at me now."

What a milestone.

When I applied for the credit and got the home loan, since I was in the industry, I knew what kind of loan I needed. But when I had my credit pulled, I found out I had more tax liens that were not discovered during my bankruptcy proceedings. Thousands and thousands and thousands of dollars *more* of tax liens popped up. To finance my house, I had to pay them off.

I could have done one of two things. I could have brought Richard back into my life and sued him. I could've gone down that rabbit hole again. I even talked to the divorce lawyer, and he gave me all the options. But the thing was, my ex had moved to Mexico with his new wife and had used money that he had been hiding from me for many years. All the money that we owed, he had taken and saved for himself. That's why he could move to Mexico and didn't have to work anymore. At the end of the day, I meant nothing to him because he was financially set.

I could have figured out a way to get ahold of him in Mexico, but I decided to just pay what was owed on my own. I didn't want him to be part of my life. That hurt me really, really badly. How could it not? I had struggled for the last three or four years since we'd divorced, and I'd moved to Austin. I had been on food stamps, working all these side jobs and hustles, cutting coupons to get fast food. You can't struggle any harder than trying to cut coupons to buy a burger. And this man had money. He just refused to give me a dime.

When all that happened, I drank more to bury more pain.

When I applied for that home loan, I said, "As much as this sucks, I'm going to pay this off." The light at the end was coming, but there was a shit-ton of hard work ahead. Knowing that made me drink. Even though I knew I needed to get my life in order and to stop being a hot mess who drank all time, I kept drinking because what he had done pissed me off.

December rolled around, and I had the hysterectomy.

In the meantime, Beatrice and I were growing further and further apart.

The house that I bought was one she wanted. I loved my house, but I wanted it for her. I made sure she loved it, too, because it was going to be our home together.

But it was becoming clear that wasn't the case.

When I bought the house on my own, Beatrice moved in with me, and shortly after, she started breaking away from me.

I didn't want to confront her about why she was growing distant because she was tender then. We had talked about adopting and fostering kids, and where before I had said I didn't think my love could carry to a child that wasn't biologically mine, she made me realize it was okay if we took in a child. We would love that child either way. We did look into it, but the cost was a little high, and we couldn't afford it. Then we decided to get her checked to see if she could be a surrogate. The plan was to use my eggs, and she would carry the child.

That's when we found out she couldn't carry a child.

I knew how she felt because she wanted children really badly, and today is a stepmom to four kids. Of course, she's wonderful at it. But at the time, instead of me being there for her, knowing what she was going through, I wasn't there for her. I did not hug her like she'd hugged me. I didn't tell her everything was going to be okay. I didn't talk to her about it. There I was watching her go through the same steps and the same emotions as I'd done five times, and I didn't know how to be there for her. What I did know that would make her temporarily happy was to give her a drink. That wasn't fair to her either.

After we left the IVF doctor and were on our way home, I asked her if she just wanted to go to the bar. She said, "Yeah." So, we got wasted that whole weekend. I don't really remember what happened. I don't know if she cried. She was a very emotional lady, so she probably did cry, but I do know I didn't hold her. I didn't ask if she wanted to talk about it. I didn't ask her if she wanted to go to therapy. I didn't say anything.

I should have been there for her. I should have immediately grabbed her and told her, "It's okay." I should have asked her: "What do you need from me? Do you want to cry on my shoulder? Do you want me to shut up? Do you want me to rub your feet?" I should have reassured her, "Whatever you need me to do, I will do." But I didn't.

I knew her heartache, how much more she probably felt than I did. Beatrice is a woman with a big heart and is more in touch with her emotions than I am. So not being emotionally there for her definitely pushed us apart.

Every time I'd been emotionally there for somebody, I'd gotten beat up. I'd gotten told I was dumb. I'd gotten taken advantage of, and nobody was there for me. That's what I knew. I knew showing love meant maybe buying her more stuff and letting her spend as much money as she wanted. Buying her physical objects was my way of showing love, but that's not what she wanted. And although she had her own way of trying to explain how she felt, I never listened because I didn't understand why she didn't get that I did love her and was there for her. I know now that my actions toward her did not match what was coming out of my mouth. I thought she had accepted that we weren't going to be Mama and Mom, and that was it. But she hadn't. Then I suspected she was going through the motions of our relationship.

We picked out the details and accents for the house together. We saw homes and got inspiration as we watched our house built. She saw me handle the tax liens, pay them off, and get a hold of my credit. I was doing all the motions and the steps, too.

She was happy, getting up early in the morning to take pictures of the build process. I was happy she was happy.

But if I would've stopped for just a second and taken a step back to assess if she was truly happy, instead of outwardly happy, I would've seen her pulling away because I wasn't emotionally there for her. I would have seen her drinking more because I was drinking more. I would have noticed her backing away further and further. She wanted love. She wanted me to hug her. She wanted reassurance. But I was to her, almost like my ex-husband was to me. She had good reason to feel so hurt since she had just received a big blow. I had, too, but the news seemed to hit her harder.

As a Christmas gift, I took her to Chicago to see one of her favorite saxophone players in his annual Christmas concert. We did a meet and greet, and I hoped it would be enough to cheer her up. The trip was a surprise, and she absolutely loved it, but two weeks before my scheduled hysterectomy. I knew something was going on with her. She was so distant from me and was definitely not the same person.

She had been someone who had shown me love and what it was like to be loved. But then there was a change. She was still loving toward me, but it was different. I didn't want to accept that things were changing, so I told myself that she was having some issues.

I reasoned that she was stressed out at work and came up with other excuses that were less scary than the truth.

Then when I had the operation, I had to face my feelings. I was trying to accept the fact that I was losing an organ that a woman's supposed to have. My hysterectomy made me feel like less of a woman. Even though I knew there was never a chance I could have actually carried a baby, and I was accepting that all my troubles were probably not my fault, it's still a piece of your body that you're supposed to have—and that I'd lost.

I went into a darker place after the surgery, which didn't help anything between us.

A woman is supposed to bring humans into this world, and I no longer had the organ to even do that. I couldn't bring kids into this world. Ever.

As I lay in bed, I thought *I'm such a fuck up that I can't even have a uterus. I had to have it taken out.* Without my uterus, the defining organ that made me a woman, I felt like I shouldn't even be around. *What was the point of existing?*

In the midst of that funk, I went back and forth on the questions of *what am I doing with my life? And, am I really, truly happy in this relationship? Even though she has been great for me, am I even happy?* Then there was the last question that was the most telling: *how can I be happy?*

I was still drinking and going through life without giving it much thought.

I'd had an amazing chance given to me in 2013 when we moved, and now it was 2016. I was self-sabotaging again. If I got caught drinking or being drunk, I would be fired on the spot. The industry was so small that it would be very difficult to get on with somebody else.

I was destroying my amazing chance.

I needed to buck up before it was too late. But that was hard.

When I had the surgery, I stayed in the hospital for a few days, but Beatrice only came and saw me once.

Something was absolutely going on with her.

Having a hysterectomy means a six-week minimum recovery time. For a full recovery, it's a good few months, but the initial recovery period has you out of work for six weeks. After you're discharged from the hospital, you can't lift anything heavier than a five-gallon milk jug. I could barely walk. You're supposed to pretty much walk only when you need to walk for the first few weeks. This was a big dent in my regular life.

My partner normally would have been there every second of the day for me. She would've worked and then been home to help me. That would've been her life until I was better.

But she wasn't there. It wasn't like her. She was different, and something was up. I just couldn't put my finger on it. Yet.

CHAPTER 11

Punch in the Gut

"Some days punch us in the gut so hard
it seems we can feel the whole
universe gasp with despair."
– Curtis Tyrone Jones

In 2017, I started a new position with a startup company. I took the position partly because it was going to give me a better work-life balance. That was the pitch they gave me when I was being recruited to this new startup builder. I bought it.

One of the things my partner and I argued about a lot was that I was always working. I was always on my phone working, too. My career consisted of working every single weekend and the majority of the holidays. Typically, she had a Monday-Friday, 9:00 to 5:00 job. So being away all the time and only having a couple of hours at the end of the day to spend with her wasn't working. Especially because instead of spending time with her, I was on my phone, *still* working. So we argued about that. Then a position came up that offered a better work-life balance. I would have more time to spend with her.

In January 2017, exactly six weeks out from my hysterectomy, I was fighting a surgical infection, but I still had to start with the new builder. So I did my first day. We had the training, and I mustered through it. It had to be done. This was going to be a better life for both of us. I knew that, and I was strong for that reason.

The more years that passed away from my ex-husband, the stronger I got. I felt a lot more confident in myself because I'd successfully purchased my first home. I'd paid off all the debt I hadn't known about until I left Richard, and the newfound tax liens as well.

Even though life was looking up in many ways, some of my habits hadn't changed at all.

That was another year of drinking and drugs (I was even dabbling in new drugs) and blowing money.

But financially, I was doing the best I'd ever done in a corporate career since I'd come to Austin, so I kept plugging along. I kept thinking as I crushed it at work: *holy shit. Imagine where I'd be if I had done this in my twenties instead of my early forties. Can you imagine what I would have accomplished in my life if I would have left him earlier?*

At the time, everything that had ever happened with Richard and with the babies was still my fault. Even though it had been medically proven that losing my babies wasn't my fault, at times, my mind blamed itself for their deaths. I prayed every single night, but in my prayers, now I asked God, *why didn't you tell me to leave?*

I had an amazing life and felt a little invincible based on what I'd pulled myself through.

Only a couple of people in my life knew about my abuse.

They didn't know everything because I kept a lot of it to myself. And while I was feeling better, I had a long way to go. Instead of looking at everything I had and all that had been given to me, I was still mentally stuck, telling myself, *wow, you are a piece of shit. You could have had this life so long ago. You are so dumb for staying.*

In February of 2017, I found out that Beatrice was having an affair. For a few months, she had been dating a woman she had met through work. Learning that she was cheating on me broke me almost harder than anything else. Harder than the divorce and finding out my ex-husband had cheated on me. That broke me a different way.

This broke my heart.

My ex-husband physically broke me ... because he was the drug. Although I was doing drugs, I had withdrawals from the person who had given me the direction I needed—because he had planned every day of my life.

I had a life with her.

And I had control of what I was doing, so it was the first time I'd felt heartbreak. When my ex-husband and I were over, I'd been a little glad we were ending, but I didn't know the direction I needed to go, so it felt like I was losing my limb.

When I found out that my female partner was cheating on me, and it was over, it knocked me over. I was weird, too, because she had always been the one who got cheated on. She knew the heartbreak she was going to give me. It brought me down into a barrel of depression. I cried and cried. When she moved out, I drank way too much. Then came the self-loathing thoughts: *How could I mess up so many times? There are so many opportunities in my life to be better, but I can't even do one thing right.*

2017 was a haze of drinking, doing drugs, and telling anyone who would listen that I was a worthless piece of shit. I was hateful to anybody who talked to me. God, I was a bitch. I don't even know how I lived through 2017. Once I drank so much, when I woke up and had to go to the bathroom, I noticed I'd thrown up on the entire bathroom wall. But I didn't remember doing that.

I was a mess, but I got up every morning. I still had to go to work. I had bills to pay and a goal in mind to be out of debt. So, I had to get up and do it. Although the few friends I had were trying to make me feel better, I felt like the worst person on earth and that there was something wrong with me.

I'd been in two major relationships in my life, and both of them had cheated on me. *There has got to be something wrong with me,* I thought. Although Beatrice had shown me love, she had also shown me heartbreak.

I still prayed every night, still thanked God for the opportunities that He'd laid before me the last couple of years. I thanked him for allowing me to move forward, even though, in reality, I was in the exact same spot I'd always been. My bank account just looked different. I didn't have the bruises on the outside either. I wasn't getting told by an outside force that I was worthless, but I was getting the same abuse because I was doing it to myself.

I had turned into the abuser and was abusing myself. Because if I couldn't hold onto two major relationships that told me I was worthless, stupid, and shouldn't think. Even after my female partner showed me *no, you're smart. You're loved.* I was still the piece of shit because she also cheated on me. That meant there was something wrong with me. She moved out. And I had to move on because she'd moved on. I'd heard she was with a woman who had kids. That was the draw for her.

It took me a while to see the truth of our breakup. I didn't see what she needed. I just hated her. That fit because I hated everything anyway.

There was nothing for me to love other than my dogs. One dog of mine, Rocky, was suffering from cancer, so I had to take him in once a week to the cancer doctor to get his treatments. Rocky was the last piece of a life that I'd had with my ex-husband because we had bought him as a puppy together. He was getting old, and I was going to have to face putting him down, which was a whole other feeling. I was saying goodbye to the last part of my life through Rocky.

Rocky was a good dog. He stuck by me, just like Mo Wrinkles, his older brother had when I'd lost five babies.

Everything that came out of my mouth was negative. I'd see a beautiful person and say, "Oh my God, look at that ugly sweater." Instead of saying, "Wow, that's a beautiful young person. Someone's doing better than me," I'd say, "They think they're so much better. They ain't nothing." Instead of saying, "Congratulations, how do you do it? Keep on pushing, girlfriend." It was "That girl's a bitch because she's doing so much better than me."

When the holidays came around in 2017, I didn't have anyone to spend them with. I had friends, sure. But not friends who wanted to spend the holidays with me. They had their own families they wanted to be with. That year, I spent the holidays alone—because who the hell wanted to spend the holidays with someone like me who didn't have anything nice to say about anyone?

And you guessed it; I was still drinking so I wouldn't feel the pain so sharply.

When I drank, I wanted to hurry up and get drunk. I wanted to hurry up and feel the effects. I wasn't going to sip on one drink for an hour and then have another one. I'd do three or four in an hour, so it would hit me like a wall. I'm not an angry drunk, but when the holidays came with families and kids, you didn't necessarily want me around.

My friends could see I was self-destructing.

They could see, I was destroying everything that had been graciously given to me. The path to a better life was sitting in front of me, and I was making the moves I wanted to make that would change my life. I had my own home. I'd paid off my debt. The only debt I had was my mortgage and a car loan. I was ahead financially, but I didn't see any of that.

Everyone could see how close to the edge I was. I know they thought, *wow, she's going to lose everything.* Of course, they were thinking that because all I was doing was drinking and dabbling in drugs.

I wouldn't have wanted to be around me on Christmas in that state. So I had Christmas on my own. I drank a few bottles of wine, had some pizza, talked to my parents on the phone, and watched movies all day.

When 2018 rolled around, it looked like I was going to do the same old bullshit. Nothing had changed. I was doing fantastically professionally and had met all my goals for 2017.

Career-wise, I was killing it. Everything I wanted to do; I was doing it. Still, I spent New Year's Eve by myself. I keep telling myself, *I know I have to get my life in order. I've got to.* But every time I told myself, *okay, I'm going to stop drinking,* it probably lasted a week.

Then I was right back to it. I always had an excuse, too. *I'm too stressed. I'm this; I'm that. I don't like the color socks I wore today. Let's have a drink.*

I also gained a lot more weight. I couldn't fit into one of my pairs of slacks. But instead of losing weight and exercising, my rationale was *let's just drink some more. Let's order another pizza. Let's have pizza for breakfast and McDonald's for lunch. Let's have whatever shit food I can find. It doesn't matter.*

But a little voice in the back of my head...God...told me: *you've prayed for me to show you the way every night for the last few years, but you keep ignoring me. Keep it up. Keep ignoring me, but I'm trying to show you. I'm here. I'm trying to pave the way for you. I'm telling you to go left, yet you keep choosing right. You're here for something better. Toni, wake up.*

God was right.

I knew by the end of 2018; if I didn't make a change, I was going to be dead soon. There was no doubt about it. But my mindset wasn't ready. I was merely tinkering with the idea. I'd say out loud to people that I needed to make a change that I needed to stop drinking and doing drugs. But the next thing I knew, I was frickin' buying drugs and drinking again.

CHAPTER 12

I Forgive You

*"To forgive is to set a prisoner free and
discover that the prisoner was you."*
– Lewis B. Smedes

2019 came around, and I wasn't happy.

If I didn't change that, I wasn't going to live much longer.

The lifestyle I was living was going to end up killing me one way or another, and I didn't want that. I wanted to be happy. I wanted to live. I wanted to experience what I'd accomplished. I'd moved to this great city and had barely seen any of it because I was too busy doing drugs, drinking, and living a bad lifestyle.

That's when I also realized I was depressed. The few times I had gone out to try to meet new people, I'd had anxiety, and I kept thinking about my past. My thoughts were relentless. *I'm doing great right now. I would probably be doing double of what I'm doing now, and all my dreams could have come true, too, if I had started in my twenties. If I had not been in that relationship. If I had joined the military...*

I relived my past almost every single day instead of realizing what I had in my future. Then I had an inspiration.

I could no longer fix my past, and I couldn't predict my future, but I could live for today. Besides, I was stronger than I thought. I was smarter, too.

One of my close friends who I had met through my relationship with my female partner moved from California to Texas to be closer to his friend. We were his family, too, so he was also coming here for us.

As I was talking to him one night, I told him how bad I felt about everything. He was one of the few people who knew enough about my past that I was sure that if I opened up a little bit more to him, he could tell me the direction I needed to go. I already knew the direction I needed to go, but I needed that validation. I needed somebody else to tell me that it was okay to move forward. And I don't know why I needed that, but I did.

That's when he introduced me to CBD, saying, "Just try it for a little bit to calm your anxiety and your mind. See if this helps and go from there." So I started taking CBD. After a couple of weeks, I did notice that I was a lot calmer. My mind was not going a million miles an hour. I didn't think so much about my past. I was also getting up and taking longer walks every morning, even though I didn't feel like doing it. I'd come home from work and would have one less glass of wine or one less cocktail.

I started telling myself every morning; *you got this.*

Every day, I took little baby steps, and every day, I struggled because every day, I still thought I'd never been good enough back when I was with Richard. And I still wasn't good enough.

Questions reeled through my mind: *why had I let myself stay? Why had I not moved forward? Why didn't I leave him sooner?*

I would think that if I would've had any one of those five children, what my life would've been like. *Would I still be together with him? Would he have been just as abusive to the child as he was to me? Would I have allowed that?*

I kept telling myself that I couldn't think that way because that life hadn't happened. I couldn't live my life as a "what if?" My friend validated to me that my ex was an asshole. He was selfish. He didn't care about anything else but himself. He also told me to think about what had happened in my life as if it were almost a blessing, like a *look at who I'm becoming today in 2019*.

I wouldn't have become who I was then and who I am today if I hadn't had my past if I hadn't had my struggles. Even though I knew that I would get hung up and think: *man, if I didn't have that past, I'd be so much greater*. But would I have been? Or would I still be exactly where I'm at today?

Everybody has a journey, and this was the path set in front of me to get to where I am today. Once I released the power that I'd allowed Richard to have in my life, I could be free. The reality was that even though he hadn't been in my life for many years, and I had no contact with him, he was still controlling me.

He was still in my head, and I had to let him go because I was never going to move forward if I didn't. If I didn't let go of all the trauma that I'd suffered, it was going to ruin me. I not only had to let it go, so it would quit holding me back, but I also had to tell myself it was not God's fault. God had been there the entire time, and I'd shut him off. That shift in my mind took a while to cement into my brain, and today, I still have to tell myself the same positive things, but it's easier now. Allowing myself to release that power and trauma of my past and actually grieve for those five babies meant I could let go at last.

Once I was able to let go of all that emotion, I could say out loud, "I forgive you." Trust me; I know that forgiving Richard doesn't mean that what happened was okay. It means for my health; I had to say it: "I forgive you."

Everyone says you can forgive, but you don't have to forget. It's a line we've all heard. But when you think about the power of forgiveness when you forgive the person that has done you wrong, it's overwhelming in a good way. I said silently; *I'm going to forgive you. I'm going to forgive the fact that, every time I lost a baby, you weren't there for me. I forgive you for not hugging me like a husband should have done. I forgive you for not telling me it was going to be okay and that you didn't tell me you loved me for me. You didn't tell me that nothing else mattered as long as I was okay. That I was important in your life. I forgive you for not telling me all of that. I forgive you for being less of a person. I forgive you for not loving me as much as I loved you. I forgive you.*

The minute that I actually meant that forgiveness, the elephant that had been sitting on my shoulders for all of those years was gone just like that.

My new healthier routine was that every morning I would get up by 5:00 am and do a little CBD. I would drink some water, get my tennis shoes on, and go work out. Once I was up for the day, I would push forward. Ever since I've been able to forgive, the change in me is night and day. The journey I have in front of me is so much different than the journey I thought I would walk. I'm happy; I'm positive. Coworkers have seen the change, and they don't know what that change is, but they've told me I'm glowing. I've lost weight; I'm excited to get up in the morning. I don't do drugs, and I don't want to.

I'm in the moment when I'm around my friends who love me. If a negative thought comes into my head (because it sometimes does; it's not like this change happened overnight), I can stop it. My friends help me stop it if I say it out loud.

I don't surround myself with negative people because the more I hear their negativity, the more it becomes my negativity. The more I hear their emotional letdowns, the more they become my emotional letdowns. I can be there for them. I can give them a hug. I can try and guide them, and I can tell them to be positive. But if they choose to continue to be in that negative space, I can't hack it. I've got to be around positive people and in a positive environment. Life is fragile, and I know I'm still fragile.

Some moments are more fragile than others. I am around the public all the time, and once in a while, I'll see a couple arguing, and it'll bring back a memory. Then I have to get out of that headspace. I'll hear a song that was one of Richard's favorites, and it will bring me back to a certain memory and time. Sometimes I don't catch it right away; sometimes, I will allow myself to have that memory, and then I'll notice my mood change.

And when I notice that I am getting off the track mentally, I literally will stop and take a deep breath. I'll close my eyes, and, as I take that deep breath, as I breathe in, I'll whisper to myself, "Let this,'"…and then I will exhale, whispering "go." Over and over again, I'll do this… "Let this…goooo…" This triggers my mind to move forward.

I now appreciate what I have and how much strength it took me to get here. I see it now, and that's my journey. Today I've accepted the losses of those five children. I have mourned them. I will never forget them, but I believe that I lost those five pregnancies for a reason.

One of those reasons is because of the abuse I was living. I don't think Richard would have hurt our children physically. Emotionally, they would have seen how he treated me, and that would have hurt them. Another reason is that God knew I could help others who hurt. I was given a resilience that not many people have. For some reason, God gave me a gift that allows me to feel the pain of others and empathize with them.

Without those losses and the abuse I suffered, I believe I would not have been able to embrace what I was meant to do. I had to suffer first. I had to dig deep into my soul and feel the radiant light I was born with. All my life, I knew I was meant to help others. I just didn't know where and how that would come about.

When I was a young child, I wanted to be a nun. I don't know why. My parents didn't push any certain religion on me. In fact, they allowed me to experience any religion or spiritual experience I wanted. As I grew older, that longing turned into me wanting to be a doctor. In high school, it turned into being in military law enforcement. In all my dreams, that urge always centered around helping and serving others.

But it wasn't until I could look at my past, forgive my past, and reflect on my past that I saw my true calling.

CHAPTER 13

I Can, and I Will

"All our dreams can come true if we
have the courage to pursue them."
– Walt Disney

Starting to tell people my story was very difficult.

As I mentioned, the only person I told was my close friend, who moved from California to Texas so we could be closer friends. None of my coworkers knew my past. Now that they know, they're all shocked.

They see a strong woman in front of them who constantly pushes forward. Someone who might be shy when you first meet her but who then opens up and pushes through that anxiety. I push forward now. I tell myself, *I got this. I can do it.* And I know I was also meant to be here to help you power through your grief.

You can use your grief to empower yourself to live the life that you want to live, whatever that life is. Because the more you allow your grief and trauma to have a hold on you, the more days of your great life you will miss out on.

Once I could forgive, accept, grieve, forgive again, and place God back into my heart, I could also accept the person I am because I had no idea what kind of individual I was. My life was so tied to everybody else's, and I didn't know who I was. Was I the type of person who loved to be around a whole lot of people and network and entertain? Or was I the type of person who was a bit of an introvert, who when out with a few friends, could be the life of the party?

I also didn't know who I was as an individual because, for most of my adult life, I became what somebody else told me I needed to be. Growing up, my parents wanted me to be a doctor. It's all they ever instilled in me. I never became a doctor, obviously. And so I felt like I'd let them down. My ex wanted me to be a certain person. Everybody wanted me to be something but had never asked me what I wanted to be. They never asked me who I was as an individual, and so I had no idea what kind of person I was until today. I now know I tend to be a little bit of an introvert.

I love being at home with my dog, surrounded by what I've accomplished; whether it's reading a book, listening to music, or hanging out by the pool, I also love hanging out with my circle of friends who have held me and been a positive force in my life. I'm in a relationship now where my partner accepts that there are times when I need to be alone because I like being alone. I know that's not for everybody. And if that's not for you, that's okay, but he accepts that I like being alone.

I like having my own space. It's not a conventional arrangement, and some people may not agree with our relationship, but it's healthy. We communicate all the time. I am not scared to tell him how I feel, whether it's good or bad.

It's the most emotionally sound relationship I have had with the most open communication. And I have it because of my past. I wouldn't have what I have today if it weren't for my past. I couldn't have the happiness I have today if, in mid-2019, I hadn't woken up and told myself, "I want to live," and then figured out what I needed to do.

I no longer want to be the woman I was in 2018 or at the beginning of 2019. I don't want to wake up so depressed and so sad that I drag through life every minute of the day. I don't want to stare at the clock and countdown to when it's time to go to sleep because I want to sleep my whole life away.

I want to be the woman who gets up and embraces the world. I thank God every single day I'm alive and have the opportunities in front of me that I do. I've got opportunities and doors opening that have been there throughout my life, but I never saw them because I was too busy blaming everything around me for the life I was given. Yet the whole time, all I needed to do was move forward.

The person I see in myself a year from now is going to be even stronger.

But you should know, having a bad past is okay. It makes you stronger and who you are today. You don't have to be ashamed.

I have a very close relationship with my parents now. I've accepted the way they are and can understand it's not that they don't want to be emotionally there. They are emotionally there for me but in their own way. They love me. They may never say it out loud, and I don't need to hear it from them anymore. But I know this is true because they show me through their actions. I couldn't see that in the past because I chose to see a different negative angle of their love. I did that because I'd surrounded myself with negativity. But again, if I didn't have that past, I wouldn't have the relationship with them that I have today.

Now, I see a bright future, and I'm excited every day to see what today is going to bring me.

I do know I suffer a little bit to this day because of the past. I don't want to say I have PTSD because it may not be that, and I haven't been diagnosed with it. But there are times that take me back like what happened the other day with the man I'm dating.

We were having a great night and goofing around. He was on one side of the room, and I was on another. Then suddenly, he ran toward me, just joking around with me, but I immediately cringed. I thought he was going to hit me. He stopped for a second and said, "Oh, my God, what's wrong?"

I looked at him and thought, *this is not about him. He's just running at me with his arms wide open because he's about to give me a big bear hug.* I had to say, "I'm sorry. I had this old reaction, and you didn't deserve that." He wasn't offended; no, he hugged me and said, "It's okay. I understand. I will never ever hurt you." And he never has.

I know there are going to be times that the universe is going to hold me back a little. There are going to be times when I'll have to sit down, breathe, and say, "No, not today. I can't let this negativity into my life."

But I'm going to choose to say I'm pushing forward. And the times when I do have the grief and think about those five pregnancies, I'll allow myself to have those memories because I'll never forget. I'll allow myself to think about those times a touch.

Then I'm going to get up and keep on walking with my head up and smiling.

I'm going to fix my crown and be the queen that I am.

CHAPTER 14

Together, We Conquer

*"Life is not about finding yourself. Life
is about creating yourself."*
– Lolly Daskal

A lot of women have gone through the same thing I have. Even if your story is not similar, we all have pain. And we all hold onto it for far too long.

I do believe I'm here and that everything I went through happened for a reason. That reason is to help you move forward because you're stuck in a spot.

Maybe you've already talked to a professional to try to get over your grief. You're aiming to move forward. You want to start living your life, pursuing your dreams, and being a better version of yourself. You want to be more present for yourself and your family's lives. If you have children, you want to be more present in their lives because you might've noticed that you're not quite there. You might still be angry. Whether you're angry at yourself,

God, or just angry in general, I want my story to help you move forward.

I've developed some courses to help more women like you.

These are the courses that have been designed to help you accept your grief and live with it without it destroying your life.

HEALING COURSES

Each course has a central theme running through it: forgiveness. When you work with me, we'll talk about understanding forgiveness and learn what forgiveness *is not* because there's a misconception of what forgiveness is.

Understanding what forgiveness is and what forgiveness is not helps you in moving forward. It helps you in letting go so you can rediscover your joy.

Each module that I've designed to help you consists of lessons and strategies that you can use to let your pain go as you finally are able to forgive.

You'll learn why forgiving is good for you and how to release your pain. You'll recognize how powerful you are and align your beliefs into releasing pain as you think your way into freedom and as you tame your pain, which ultimately helps you change your behavior.

In each of these modules and lessons, we'll offer a summary and a reflection as well.

In my Healing From Emotional Trauma Course, you'll learn:

• Why forgiveness is crucial to your mental, emotional, and physical health

• How childhood beliefs can interfere with releasing the past

• You have the power within you to release the past

• Forgiveness brings freedom

- Strategies to assist you in forgiving and letting go

In a separate course, *Becoming Your Beautiful Authentic Self*, I created ways for you to discover new joys as you learn to let go of living the way that others think you should. You'll learn how to:

- Discover who you really are
- Find out your true passions
- Build your self-esteem
- Let go of past mistakes and accept yourself
- Break free from crippling self-doubts
- Embrace your individuality
- Love yourself
- Find your life purpose
- Show the world the real you
- Create a joyful life by living authentically

We'll construct a healthy self-image by re-building you and your self-esteem as we push you to be proactive to increase your satisfaction in life. You'll have conversations about *who do you want to be?* Accepting yourself gives you a higher self-esteem, so it is unmistakable and unshakeable. It is so exciting to learn how to get there.

You'll discover that hiding and pushing your voice away that wants to reinforce self-doubt is not acceptable. We focus on this because we want you to have a healthy self-image so you can accept yourself.

In my second relationship, I discovered that I loved my girlfriend, but I didn't love myself. In that way, I couldn't really give her the love that she deserved.

That's why we'll also talk about how to stop seeking approval from other people. Take heart because this is a flaw that a lot of people have. The truth is that we do certain things because we want the approval of the people around us, and we need to stop seeking it.

Approval needs to come from ourselves. To achieve this state, we must believe in the power of ourselves and stop comparing ourselves to others.

The keys to reaching these goals are to believe in ourselves, to love ourselves, to love our bodies, and to love our emotional, intellectual, and spiritual selves.

Parts of the courses pertain to determining your life purpose. You'll learn how to unlock your true life's calling and tap into the power of writing and meditating as you focus on what you are meant to do.

We'll also delve into living authentically. Being authentic and yourself is an allegiance to your true personality.

You will learn to activate the courage to express your feelings and present them honestly. You'll tap into the power of the inner voice—that inner strength that you've been pushing down and refusing to let out. We're going to help you uncover the courage to do it all.

Additionally, you'll learn how to set life priorities and live by them, how to reveal your true personality, and find the courage to express your feelings, and how to present yourself honestly.

In the years that I was married, I presented to the public somebody else who wasn't me, who was living a different life behind the scenes.

I want you to live as your true self and resist having a public persona while being somebody else in the background. That's not living authentically.

Authentic living means how you live in the background is how you live in public. There is no difference.

When you walk through the front door of your house, you're going to be the same person as you were when you were outside.

These courses are designed to specifically walk you through them step by step. When you're done with the modules and all the lessons, I want you to feel the strength of yourself.

You may not be shouting from the rooftops; you might simply take one step forward that you were scared to take.

That's perfect.

These courses are all about moving forward, and if that means taking one step, that is a step to be proud of!

If you're interested in learning more about these courses and how you can unleash the real self you are meant to be, please get in touch with me in one of the following ways:

• You can look me up on Facebook at Toni Giddley. Or, find me on Instagram @Toni_Giddley.

• You can find our private Facebook Group called Restore Your Life. Once you join the courses, you'll be part of the Facebook Group. This is a no-judgment zone and a community that will help you connect with one another. I guarantee somebody else is experiencing grief right along with you—that they are in the same position, trying to move forward. This group encourages each other to resist becoming the person we were in the past and to move forward to become the person we know we can be in the future. Today we are happy. Tomorrow we're going to be even happier. That's what the group is for.

• Connect with me on our website: ToniGiddleyLifeCoach.com.

One of my favorite people to read about and research is Abraham Lincoln. I've always been enthralled by him. He once said, "I walk slowly, but I never walk backward." I read that quote years ago when my mother bought me a book about him. He lived his life that way. And I live my life that way today.

I rediscovered that quote not long ago, and it touched me. Even if a day is a challenge, I will never walk backward. That's not an option for me, and it's not an option for you.

Walking slowly forward will give you the empowerment and love you need to start you on the path to your right journey.

That's what I encourage you to do now and always: walk slowly and never look back.

ACKNOWLEDGMENTS

Special thanks to Shelby Odell and Brandon Wigglesworth. You two have been my rock and inspiration in my life. I am forever grateful to have found such amazing friends.

Brandon has never held back his honest truth from me.

Shelby is wise beyond her years.

My mother who has, in her own way, shown and taught me how to be a strong woman. She is a no-holds-barred force of nature. Today, I understand why she was so hard on me. I have always had inner strength. I just had to believe in myself. Secretly, she is my hero.

My father, who has never judged me and has one of the purest hearts. No matter if I am sad, happy, or pissed off, this man will tell one of the worst Dad jokes you've ever heard that will make you laugh till you cry.

Steve Forbes of Exit King Realty in Sarasota, FL. I am forever thankful for your help when I needed it the most. You never knew how much my life changed because of you.

And, as silly as it sounds, my four dogs; Mo'Wrinkles, Rocky

Bear, Titus, and George Randolph Bugsy. All are now at the Rainbow Bridge. If it wasn't for the unconditional love of these dogs, I would not have been able to keep going. Needing to take care of them really meant they were taking care of me. Today, we have Princess Meko and Odin Lorraine. If you ever are looking for a new fur-baby, please consider looking at your local shelter.

The information contained within both the www.tonigiddleylifecoach.com website and the *But First, You Must Forgive* book is not a substitute for professional advice such as seeking a medical doctor, psychiatrist, or counselor. The information provided by www.tonigiddleylifecoach.com and the *But First, You Must Forgive* book does not constitute legal or professional advice, nor is it intended to.

Diagnosing psychological or medical conditions is for trained medical professionals (physicians and therapists); it is not for a life coach to do.

Business coaching is not a substitute for engaging the services of a CPA or Attorney.

Any decisions you make, and the consequences thereof are your own. Under no circumstances can you hold www.tonigiddleylifecoach.com and the book *But First, You Must Forgive* liable for any actions that you take.

You agree that under any circumstances, you will not hold www.tonigiddleylifecoach.com, Toni Giddley LLC, its employees of www.tonigiddleylifecoach.com or Toni Giddley LLC liable for any loss or cost incurred by you, or any person related or associated with you, as a result of materials techniques, or coaching, offered by www.tonigiddleylifecoach.com or the book, *But First, You Must Forgive.*

Results are not guaranteed.

www.tonigiddleylifecoach.com and the book, *But, First You Must Forgive,* holds no responsibility for the actions, choices, or decisions taken or made by you.

The owner of and any contributors to www.tonigiddleylifecoach.com and the book, *But, First You Must Forgive,* accepts no responsibility or liability whatsoever for any harm—real or imagined—from the use or dissemination of information contained herein.

If these terms are not agreeable, do not engage the services.

By engaging any/all of the services of the www.tonigiddleyifecoach.com website and coaching business and reading the book *But, First You Must Forgive,* you have agreed to all terms and conditions.

I'm a badass because I am a survivor who never gave up.

I grew up in a military family. An only child and lonely. My mother was meaner than cat piss and was quick with her hand. One bad move, and she would smack me with a quickness. Her words cut me deep. I learned fast that words hurt deeper than any physical violence.

My father was the man with a golden heart. He was always my hero. He wasn't around much growing up, not because he didn't want to be, but because the military sent him away a lot. When he was home, I was stuck to him like glue.

When I was a teenager, I gave my parents a run for their money. I was a little shit that caused my parents more gray hair than they needed. I cut school, snuck out of the house, stole my parents' car, and defied the rules any way I could. It didn't matter what my parents did to get me in line. I was bound and determined to do the complete opposite.

When I was eighteen, I met a guy and was out my parents' door. He was bad news from the start. For the next eighteen years, he was abusive. The physical part took a toll on my body. The emotional part affected me to my soul. After too many years of hearing how I was worthless and stupid, I believed it. I lost my self-worth and my identity. I didn't know how to function without being told what to do.

In those years with my ex-husband, I became pregnant five times. I lost all five of those beautiful beings—three of them from ectopic pregnancies, two from miscarriages. I experienced each loss alone. At each doctor's appointment and each treatment, I was alone.

After one brutal beating, I was done. I found the courage to rip apart from my ex and start my life over.

It took six years to find my way to where I am today.

I was homeless and begged for money from family and friends. I filed for bankruptcy, became a drug addict, drank from sunup until I passed out, and in the process, gained 100lbs. My life spiraled as I slowly killed myself.

In 2019, I looked in the mirror and didn't like what I'd turned into. I was allowing my past to define who I could become in the future. I was allowing the words of hate spewed at me for so long to define my everyday life. I knew I was better than the girl looking back at me in the mirror.

I know you are, too.

You are not alone.

I'm Toni Giddley, and it's nice to meet you.

www.ingramcontent.com/pod-product-compliance
Lightning Source LLC
Chambersburg PA
CBHW061540120726
48001CB00004B/1641